MEMORI

OF A

SEA GIPSY

About growing up in

wartime Belfast

and

life as a freelance

Radio Officer

on board

British, Greek and

Norwegian ships.

Author

DEREK PETERS

FOREWORD

Derek Peters was a young child when war broke out, but, reading this book, one gathers the impression that he wishes he'd been born sooner, so that he could have seen the action at first hand. He was possessed of a restless and inquisitive nature, which led him to go to sea in the early '50s, as a radio officer, first on Marconi's list, then as a free-lance. He has a good eye and ear, his experiences on a variety of ships, under many flags, are here set down with sometimes humorous, sometimes biting accuracy, and, in these pages he recreates for us a world that is long gone, the times when Liverpool was a bustling seaport; when ships by the dozen had to wait in line for berths, in Belfast Lough, and on Cardiff Roads.

The world of the radio operator is one that I know well, although my experience was gained in an aeroplane, but wireless operators were a special breed, people who had mastered a different craft - the sending of fast and accurate morse code tranmissions. All messages were sent within a procedural code, known as the Q code, but often, when the transmission was over, there came the morse warble that carried a personal, shortened message of goodwill from an operator that one was likely never to meet in person. When I was on wartime operations, perhaps sending a sighting report of an enemy ship, the ground station, after acknowledging, would have sent 'glom' - good luck, old man, and it was truly meant.

Derek Peters was one of the brotherhood, and he manages the difficult job of bringing the general reader into this esoteric and very private world, with admirable ease.

The experiences that he recounts are about places: fascinating, exotic, sometimes lively, often deadly dull places, in the USA, Canada, Poland, South America, New Zealand, but the strength of the book lies in Peters' descriptions of the people he met in those places - particularly the ladies. He was a single young man in his early 20's, just in from the sea, but relationships that often led to the bedroom are handled with exactly the right blend of sensitivity and an honesty as refreshing as a warm shower. It should also be said that the author is one of the few merchant seamen I have met who was interested enough in the countries he visited to explore them for miles beyond the nearest pub or night club.

I greatly enjoyed reading this, Mr Peters' first book. In particular, I enjoyed the way in which he described the oddball characters with whom he found himself shipmates, but, over and above every other treat in the story, I enjoyed my return to the days when the United Kingdom had a merchant fleet that made its citizens proud, the days when there was scarcely a port in the wide world that didn't have, alongside one of its jetties, a ship proudly flying the Red Duster.

Sam McAughtry

RECOLLECTIONS OF YOUTH

In 1932 Belfast was in a trough of a depression, with grass growing on the great slipways of Harland and Wolff's shipyard, and fine shipyard craftsmen digging up the cobblestones of the city's back entries in the Outdoor Relief Scheme. I was born that year and knew nothing of this except hearsay. I do remember however, when I was about three years old, my father asking the tradesmen, who had just finished our kitchen extension, to 'make their number.' 'Nothing, Mr Peters,' one workman said, 'if you could only speak for us somewhere and get us a job'. My father of course paid the men and I am sure he asked around to try and get jobs, but it is seared into my memory how desperate the men must have been to get work.

My father was in fact a very humble constable in the Royal Ulster Constabulary, our provincial police force. Things must have been very bad indeed for the poor men to hope that my father could help them, as he himself hated police work but was totally unequipped to get another job.

The Castlereagh Road in East Belfast was a neat tree-lined road, semi-villas lining in uniform respectability towards the rolling rim of the Castlereagh Hills. Civil servants, policemen, shopkeepers and clerks, indeed anyone financially secure enough to raise a mortgage, pushed their way out of the Victorian backstreets of East Belfast. Orangefield Estate was built in neat lines of semi-detatched villas, each one with a separate and distinctive feature to show the individuality of its owner, newly escaped from the indistinguishable serried ranks of the 'back-to-back' of the inner city.

Life centered around the churches on the new estate, all two of them, the Church of Ireland and the Presbyterian. The two Catholic families of Southern Irish policemen, who took the opportunity to finish their service in Northern Ireland after the partition settlement in 1922, had to walk over to the new Chapel in Willowfield on the Woodstock Road.

We children went to Sunday School, joined the Wolfcubs, and dutifully received our prizes at Christmas for being good children. Our elders sported themselves at the Badminton Club and the Amateur Dramatic Society in the name of Christ. That was at the Church of Ireland or Anglicans; the Presbyterians didn't hold with play acting or sports connected with the church.

Indeed, they did have mixed classes for teenagers which drew attendance from both congregations. The teenagers, however, seemed more interested in each other than the Bible. My mother produced for the dramatic society in the Church of Ireland and I know that in a later age she would have been a professional theatre person. As it was, she taught shorthand and typing and managed to teach herself Spanish, without having the opportunity to use it until war came. Like most of her generation, she never managed to move outside these islands in her lifetime.

My early life was cocooned in a safe world of visits to relatives, the Wolfcubs and tennis club parties for the children. The R.U.C. Tennis Club was at the end of Grand Parade, where we lived, and it also hosted the R.U.C. tug-of-war team. I have distinct memories of big West of Ireland men, their uniform tunics off, their braces dangling, as they sweated and cursed as they pulled. 'Heave now, God blast yee' would ring out as they gained a few inches on the opposing team.

Father came and went at odd hours, presumably harrassing the criminals of East Belfast, and one memorable time he took the Police Barracks at Willowfield to see the armoury lined with .303 Lee Enfield rifles. This institution was presided over by big kindly men with West of Ireland accents, like himself, for father was born in a police barracks in County Clare, where his father was the local Sergeant. One of these men, now retired, lived around the corner from us. He was a huge man, was Head Constable Roe, with an enormous beer belly. He waddled rather than walked, hailing all he knew with sentences in triplicate. 'How are you? How are you? How are you?' he would boom. 'Tis cold, tis cold, tis cold.' 'Tell your father to put on his winter drawers, his drawers, his drawers.' When he met my mother he would recite the same litany, this time referring to my father as 'Dixie', the South of Ireland sobriquet for Richard.

School time came at five years old, and I was duly taken down Ladas Drive and up Daddy Winker's Lane to Harding Memorial School. One entrance was for boys and the other for girls, although we both sat together once inside. We recited our arithmetic tables, practiced our alphabets and said our prayers, all in unison. My one bad memory of the place is of being kept waiting at the kerb, returning from lunch, as the headmaster chatted to the policeman who was supposed to show us across the Cregagh Road. Of course I was late back to class and was sent to the same headmaster who promptly gave me two stinging slaps on the hand for being late. The injustice of this and my own lack of ability to explain matters gave rise to an intense hatred of the man for the rest of my time at school.

School was uneventful until the war came in 1939 and then all was changed utterly. First of all we were taught how to knit, boys and girls both. We clicked away, knitting pink, green and purple squares, which we duly handed up to the teacher to make into bedcovers for the troops. I had visions of rows of soldiers in the trenches, bedding down for the night under brightly coloured knitted patchwork bedspreads. I have often wondered what actually happened to those bedspreads. Next came the gasmasks. These were contained in cardboard boxes and had to be carried everywhere, and in the manner of children we played with them, obliterating all thoughts of the grim purpose for which they were issued.

My uncle was a sergeant in the local Searchlight Unit of the Territorial Army, so he was mobilized and sent to France, while another uncle who was a freshly qualified medical doctor joined the R.A.M.C. There was a family of four boys and one daughter in the house next door. Three of the boys joined the Royal Navy and the daughter joined the A.T.S. as the women's army was then known. The fourth son, who had a good job in the aircraft factory, was expelled from the household for refusing to enlist. The Crawford family were indeed fiercely loyal, all belonging to the Orange Order. At the twelfth of July, which is the anniversary of the Protestant victory at the battle of the Boyne, I saw the three Crawford boys walk in the March, their Royal Navy uniforms bedecked with Orange collarettes which was strictly against Kings regulations, I am sure. Mrs Crawford berated all men of military age who weren't in uniform. One unfortunate Salvation Army collector was greeted with 'Why aren't you in the real army?' 'Thou shalt not kill', said the salvationist, to which Mrs Crawford retorted, 'Thou shalt not shite.'

Mrs Crawford had constant visits from women garbed in shawls and carrying buckets. Apparently she ordered coal from the Co-op on her account, which she sold to her former neighbours at a shilling a bucket. The Co-op quarterly account sometimes presented difficulties, but Mrs Crawford's business disappeared with the war and the resulting prosperity.

Czeckoslovakia and Poland were on everyone's lips in September 1939. We children heard the war prognostications from the adults and studied the war map courtesy of the Daily Express. I reckoned that the map areas of Britain, France and Poland exceeded that of Germany. This fact, plus the more pleasing and symmetrical shape of the British army helmet, convinced me that the allies would win the war. My father received his black steel helmet with R.U.C. written on it, while my mother found her knowledge of the Spanish language afforded her employment in the civil censorship. All references to the war in private mail were to be blue pencilled. Meanwhile at Harding Memorial, junior infants knitted away furiously. In spite of this, Poland fell and then France, and I gathered from the talk at the table that the Ulster Anti-Aircraft Brigade were abandoned by their officers and that the N.C.O's and men had to make their way on foot to Dunkirk.

Uncle George swam out to the rescue boats from the beaches, landed at Dover and promptly put in for a transfer to the R.A.F. Uncle George had been a shop assistant in his cousin's shop and had been turned down for the R.U.C. because of a hammer toe. At twenty nine years old, six foot two and darkly handsome, he was my grandmother's pride and joy. He was accepted for aircrew training and was sent to Canada. Grandfather Peters' elder brother had already emigrated to Canada where, in Winnipeg, he was raising, from all accounts, a large rumbustious brood. My father's own family was famed for rows and feuds, with shifting alliances amongst the five sisters. The story goes that when Uncle George appeared in the Winnipeg street where the Canadian Peters family lived, being unsure of the correct street number, he stopped at a house from where the sounds of a domestic quarrel were emitting and, sure enough, it was the Peters' household.

Later on in the war, what appeared to be Uncle George in Canadian Naval uniform arrived at our door in Belfast, but it turned out to be one of the Canadian cousins who was stationed at Londonderry. The Peters' clan have a very distinctive look, dark, long nosed and tall, and there was no mistaking him for anything else. Four decades later, Stalin's daughter Svetlana married an American architect named Peters, which is I suppose a common enough name in America, but when I saw his picture on T.V. I could see that he had the same Peters look and build. I have wondered since, if he could have been one of the offspring of the Canadian Peters family. George Peters was shot down on his twenty-ninth mission over Germany and is buried in the British Military Cemetary in Duisburg. My grandmother wore George's R.A.F. winged emblem pinned to her black mourning dress until she died about fourteen years later.

Unlike the working class Crawfords, middle class Orangefield did not rush to join the colours. The slaughter at the Somme in 1916, when General Haig sent the flower of Ulster's manhood into the teeth of the German machine guns had destroyed the peoples' trust in Generals. People were reluctant to be cannon fodder again. There was a memory of five thousand telegrams delivered from the G.P.O. notifying the relatives of the death of their sons and husbands at the battle of the Somme. These were only the fallen before lunchtime at Thiepval Wood. The right of the Generals to play fast and loose with people's lives was being queried. Later in the war, the youths finishing school at Belfast Inst. where I attended, enlisted in great numbers to the R.A.F. where the romantic cachet of aircrew was much in evidence.

The war brought blackened windows, women at work, the Home Guard and, later on in 1941, the German Blitz on Belfast. The war maps now included Africa and Asia, and my analysis of the situation stated that the map areas coloured red and blue, signifying the British and French empires outmapped the German and Italian orange mapped areas.

In that grim time after Dunkirk and before Germany attacked the Soviet Union, there was much talk of the Germans landing in Southern Ireland, which was then officially known as Eire, but invariably called 'The Free State' after its first official name of the Irish Free State. It later became The Republic of Ireland and now prefers to be known as plain Ireland. But to those in Northern Ireland and those who live along the southern side of the border, it will always be the simple two syllable 'Freestate'. By this time I realised that the Catholic citizens of our Province were more numerous than just the MacDermots and the Hannigans. I knew by then that there were breaches of the blackout regulations on the Falls Road, which was the main Catholic area in Belfast. Britain was isolated, but still a hard nut to crack, and would be defended by a reasonably effective re-mustered army, an as yet untouched Navy, and an Airforce that was rapidly gaining ascendency of the skies.

The Free State however was neutral, really neutral, in that it even maintained a German Embassy. The then Prime Minister of Eire, Mr De Valera, showed his true colours at the end of the war when he went personally to the German Embassy to give his condolances to the ambassador on the death of Hitler. He was the only leader in the world to do this. The small Irish army was short of everything it needed and its soldiers were deserting in droves, selling their uniforms in the border town of Newry, and going to Belfast to join the British Forces. We heard rumours that the Germans had landed in Cork and were heading north, but these turned out to be mobilisation tests. I felt sorry for the Free State, their area on the map was very small and apparently their deserting soldiers' uniforms only fetched five shillings in Newry.

Prior to the war, my parents had rented a charming weekend country cottage on the slopes of the Mourne mountains, near Newcastle in County Down. The cottage had walls of three foot granite and a slab stone floor, a fireplace made from granite slabs with a swinging crook for the kettle. The Irish Sea seemed to flow up to the stone dyke at the edge of the field. The splendid shadow-blue massifs of Slieve Donard and Slieve-na-Garragh loomed across the corrugated iron roof. The gentle rushing sound of the Bloody Bridge river was forever in our ears. We had the last house but one on a loney leading to the quarries on the Donard side. The last house on the loney belonged to the O'Neill family and the house was built by Felix from granite blocks, hewn by himself from the quarry. He raised a two-story slated house that commanded a view of the coast that well rewarded the half mile walk to it. Felix hacked half-a-dozen fields out of the slopes of Slieve-na-Garragh, painstakenly building the dykes from the rock he had cleared. The man was lean and leathery, scorned tobacco and alcohol and was the embodiment of the indomitable Irish I would prefer to remember.

Felix kept a few cattle on his hard won fields and sheep on the mountain. He also kept a pony and trap which he would harness to go to the fair at Castlewellan and Dundrum. There was no gas or electricity available, all the heating being provided by turf from the bog on Donard which had to be brought down by donkeys with panniers, called creels. Not having a radio, the O'Neill family relied on us for news of the world outside. They christened their feuding cousin and neighbour 'Hitler' when it got through to them that Hitler was the baddie on the world scene. This was a source of great confusion to myself, as I never knew whether it was the German Fuhrer or Felix's cousin who had tumbled the ditch and allowed Felix's sheep to wander. The O'Neill's spontaneous wit, unvarnished logic and bare handed battle with poverty taught me much, which as a child I would never have learnt in the bourgeois cocoon of the Castlereagh Road. The O'Neill children, my brother and myself played endless games amongst the pools and rocks of the Bloody Bridge river, and skittered down the steep fields on Felix's iron shod sledge, called a slipe. This artefact was used to draw the granite slabs for the house from the quarry on Donard. The only thing I have seen like it since is the sledge with a wicker basket on top which is used to hurtle the tourists down the mountain in Madeira.

Our arrival at the weekend was the signal for Mrs O'Neill to appear at the door to listen to the radio. 'Does it talk all the time?' she said, sotto voce, when she first heard it. When you think about it, radio-telephony is a bit of a mystery. You can't feel it or see it, so where does it come from? Mrs O'Neill decided logically enough that it must come from the box.

The O'Neills were Catholics, and early contact with them barricaded my mind from that great enemy of life, religious bigotry. The O'Neill family managed to exist on about ten acres, but the lower two-room cottage on the lane was the home of a prolific Protestant family who were landless. They were good neighbours to each other and the Lowry children often helped the O'Neills with the potatoes or the corn when the harvest was ready. The idea abroad about the 'Protestant' landlord and the poor 'Catholic' tenants would have appeared as a poor joke to the Lowrys if they had known of it. Poverty stalked both communities and still does, and when I hear Catholic nationalist politicians in Ulster, I remember the Lowrys and the thousands like them.

My grandfather once came to stay in our cottage in the Mournes. He was a huge, cadaverous man, ascerbic with it, and in his mid-seventies. On arrival, he promptly went down with a raging 'flu. My brother and myself were entrusted with his care until he was well enough to return to Belfast. We heated a brick in the open fire, wrapped it in an old blanket and placed the brick in his bed. Granda's teeth still chattered, so we heated the brick again until it glowed red. He still complained of the cold, but in ten minutes there was smoke billowing from the bed with the old man complaining all the while of the cold. We put the fire out and eventually he got better and made his way down the lane to get the bus for Belfast. On the way he met Mrs O'Neill, 'I hope you'll soon come back to Bloody Bridge again, sir', she civilly greeted him. 'Indeed, by Christ, I won't,' he swore.

UNCLE GEORGE AND GRANDMOTHER PETERS

THE BLITZ ON BELFAST

For most of the war, Northern Ireland acted as a secure manufacturing base and training ground for various armies, a Godsend to the Navy and Merchant Navy, now denied the use of Eire's ports. Destroyer escorts to the convoys of merchant ships saved twelve precious hours steaming by using Londonderry. President Roosevelt wanted Churchill to seize the Eire ports to give another twelve hours' advantage to the escorts and submarine hunters, but Churchill, having had his fingers burned by Irish politics before, desisted. So the bodies of drowned allied seamen washing up on the shores of the West of Ireland were the real price of Irish neutrality in the war against fascism. It is interesting to note that George Bernard Shaw, the great Irish writer, had written to H.G.Wells about the U.S.S.R. seizing the northern approaches to Leningrad from Finland at this time. This action undoubtedly saved Leningrad from the Germans and lost Hitler the war. Shaw wrote that Southern Ireland was England's Finland and that England should seize the southern ports for the duration, in the name of humanity and democracy. Had Churchill had the same determination as Stalin, the war would have been shortened by a year, and millions of holocaust victims would have been saved from the gas chambers.

Because of distance Belfast seemed secure against air attacks, but the importance to the allied cause of the aircraft factory and the shipyard caused Goering to risk his pilots on the long round journey. One night in April 1941 the Luftwaffe struck. The civil defences were completely unprepared, the local Territorial Army anti-aircraft regiment had been sent to India as infantry, and only six anti-aircraft guns remained in the city. The air raid warning went out as far as I can remember at about ten p.m. and the noise started. Mother brought us downstairs and placed us under the stout oak table in the dining room. The cacophany of noise was terrifying, the pump-pump of ack-ack guns were the drumbeats to the drone of the bombers and the crash of the explosions.

At eight years old I knew we could die at any moment and the best approach seemed to be to crouch in the foetal position and hope for the best. With hindsight it would have been more prudent to flee the city altogether. We were only half a mile from the open country and every step would have us further away from danger. My father and brother stood in the yard and watched the illuminations. My brother who was ten seemed impervious to fear and kept up a running commentary on where the bombs were falling. The German bombers had it all their own way and none were shot down. There was a far fetched rumour circulating later that one of the sons of a Belfast Italian ice-cream family had guided them over the city. Many decades later I read that some of the family concerned had been active fascists and had indeed returned to Italy to help the fascist war effort. The Germans had the help of the I.R.A. who spied out the positions of the anti-aircraft defences for them, according to Paddy Devlin the Labour politician, who was an I.R.A. member at the time. However, the people of Belfast were afforded better protection than the brick shelters provided by the Government. I still remember the streams of working class families with push bikes, carts and prams heading up the Castlereagh Road to the safety of the Castlereagh Hills the next night. The people bedded down in the fields, hoping it would not rain, and returned next morning. After the second blitz, my uncle, who was on leave from the Army, whisked us away to the cottage in the Mournes in his old Austin car with the dickey seat at the back. What is now the Knock duel carriageway was then a winding country road escarping the first ridge of the Castlereagh Hills. From that open back seat I could see a mass of flames and plumes of black smoke rising from the city centre. It was the last we were to see of Belfast for a year. The bombing raids followed for another week. From the cottage at Bloody Bridge, we could hear the planes droning up the Irish sea, guided by the lights of neutral Eire, crossing over St. John's Point where desultory ack-ack fire would erupt from the battery beside the lighthouse. In a few seconds we could hear the muffled sound of explosions in Belfast thirty miles away.

All told, the bombs on Belfast caused two thousand casualties, which was part of the price to pay for membership of the United Kingdom. Most of the damage was to civilian housing; the shipyard and the aircraft factory were also damaged but were soon back in production. My father told me that the Blitz put paid to the 'IRA Help Germany Campaign' which encouraged people to leave lights on in the attic etc. After the Blitz there was no need for the air-raid wardens to shout 'Put out that light.'

There is no doubt in my mind that the decision to leave Belfast undefended was a dereliction of the Government's duty to the people of Ulster. The casualties suffered in Belfast were the greatest of any single air-raid in the U.K. and the mortuaries were so full of bodies that the public baths had to be requisitioned to cope with the overflow. About sixty bodies were unidentified and were buried in a mass grave in the city cemetery.

The Dublin Fire Brigade raced north to help and indeed they had plenty of time to do so, as the raid went on till dawn. A story is told of a man being dug out of the rubble by the Dublin firemen and on hearing the strong Dublin accent said: 'That must have been a hell of a bomb, to blow me all the way to Dublin.'

My brother, my mother and myself settled into a new life in the cottage and soon adapted to a life of well-drawn water, paraffin lamps and a one room country school. Mother rose at six a.m., cycled into Newcastle where she left her bike and caught the seven a.m. train to Belfast. It was a very long day for her as she did not return until seven forty-five at night. Eventually, she had to take the decision to board us out with families and stay herself in Belfast with my father. The first family we were boarded with were a professional couple in Rostrevor, which is an idyllic part of the Mournes, and while I can say that I adjusted well considering the circumstances, my brother reacted to the separation by being exceedingly cheeky to the people. His strategem worked, for the people wanted rid of us after two months. This happened again with a Protestant fundamentalist family we were boarded with in Richhill, Co. Armagh. On the day that the man was due to preach in the gospel hall, Dermot told him he wouldn't be able to see over the pulpit. The man indeed lacked inches, and his fury was such that he abandoned all attempts to proselytise, and told our parents to take us away as soon as possible. Our last stop was the Royal School, Armagh, where we were boarded with different families whose sons also attended the school. I can't say that I was happy during that period, as there was always the feeling that I did not belong. The arrangement lasted until the following Christmas when it seemed that, with the Americans entering the war, Belfast was not such an important industrial target anymore.

GROWING UP IN WARTIME BELFAST

Both my grandfathers had been sergeants in the old Royal Irish Constabulary, which was disbanded in 1922 when the Irish Free State seceded from the United Kingdom. Both were second sons of Protestant farmers in the South of Ireland. They both opted to take their families to live in Belfast, reckoning, quite rightly as it turned out, that the new Free State would evolve into a claustrophobic, clerically dominated state where they would not be welcome. Ex R.I.C. members who were Catholics found no difficulty in adopting to the new regime in the South, as generally there was no rancour towards the force, in spite of the spate of hate-inspired memoirs from former gunmen who were now a power in the land. 'My Fight For Freedom' by Dan Breen is an example of this, where Breen alleged that he started the squalid guerrilla war by shooting in cold blood an unsuspecting R.I.C. constable escorting explosives to a quarry. All that both grandfathers had in common apparently was that they detested each other, mainly because Grandfather Peters lacked ambition and had refused promotion in order to remain Depot Sergeant at R.I.C. Depot, Phoenix Park in Dublin. His duties there by all accounts were not very onerous, consisting solely of lighting the gas under the clock in the officers' mess. Eventually, he discovered that the jet was not discernible during daylight hours, so he left it on all the time. He was a fine figure of a man in the Victorian mode, six foot three inches tall, with broad shoulders, dark good looks and a waxed moustache. Perhaps the R.I.C. officers thought that just standing about in his neatly pressed uniform was a good example to the recruits. Eventually he was transferred to County Clare where my father was born.

The family lived in the barracks and as each child turned fourteen, it had to leave the married quarters. This was the time that De Valera was MP for County Clare, and with all the nationalist hysteria about, Granda Peters sent his ten children to Belfast as they came of age. The Protestant population of the Free State was then around three hundred thousand and, as I write, it is now in the region of one hundred thousand. The reason for this, I believe, lies in the experience of my own family, they being aware of hostility and the suffocating atmosphere of Catholic religiosity. No book has yet been published to my knowledge of this demographic phenomenon, so perhaps some researcher will undertake such a project.

Both my parents' families were keen on education so sent my brother and myself to the Belfast 'Inst.' at a cost of £24 per annum each. This represented two months' pay for my father, so it was a big sacrifice for him. At 'Inst' my brother made a name for himself by ignoring any school rule which did not suit him. His name was called out every Friday school meeting for detention on Saturday morning, and he never went. He would light up a cigarette going out of the school gates and refused to own, never mind wear, a school cap. That Dermot, my brother, should choose the Army, with its emphasis on discipline for a career seems strange, but that is what he did, and indeed, all through his youth he never considered anything else.

'Inst', being a beautiful Georgian building right in the centre of Belfast, had a long tradition of secular scholarship which, I suppose, was unique in Belfast, where most grammar schools were attached to some church or other. It was a very bourgeois institution, most of the boys being scions of the 'merchant princes' and professional classes of Belfast. There were a number of boys I had known at the elementary school before the Blitz. Looking back, I remember that these boys were the brightest but a fair proportion of them left school before they were eighteen to take up employment, mostly in offices. Some of the masters at 'Inst' were quite eccentric; one of them, who later became British Consul in Valparaiso in Chile, used to write letters to the devil, screw them up into a bunsen burner and set fire to them. My only interest was in History and English at which I won several prizes. I did, however, learn the rudiments of French, German and Spanish which stood me in good stead in my later career in the Merchant Navy. Having failed to keep up with the maths lessons, I sank deeper and deeper into the morass of incomprehension, until I finally abandoned the struggle to make any sense of it.

I left school at sixteen and took a job in an office because I never had any money to do the things teenagers liked to do. It was a mistake that I painfully found out not many months afterwards when the dull, repetitive nature bore down on me. I was, however, caught with a great enthusiasm for hiking and camping in the mountains, and in company of older friends developed a deep love for the countryside. The railway to Newcastle, Co. Down, was operating in those days and the journey there and back was a great occasion, with dozens of rucksack-laden youths singing, joking and relating the tales of their fortunes and misfortunes in the mountains.

We met English, Scottish and Southern Irish people in the youth hostels, and would sit up singing folk songs around the hostel fire. Some of my friends who were apprentice craftsmen used to go to Europe hitch-hiking for entire summers when they had served their apprenticeship. Home, being on part of an island, gave us all a great curiosity about the outside world, coupled with the exuberance of youth and the love of nature. Today there are very few young people in the mountains and the availability of cars means that they travel in sealed boxes, cut off from the great social travelling in trains that we knew.

Another of my interests was the Territorial Army, which was re-formed in 1948. I joined the sixth battalion of the Royal Ulster Rifles in Victoria Barracks and became an enthusiastic, if under-age, soldier at the age of sixteen. Our regular army instructors were grizzled veterans of the Second World War who were coming up to retirement and given local postings. The regimental sergeant major was a wee banty cock of a man; his uniform pressed and spotless, his boots like mirrors, his brasses polished like gold and he was entitled to wear an officer's green bonnet and regimental swagger stick. His commands were delivered in a high staccato squeal, followed by a tirade of good natured abuse. The command 'rifles', delivered 'rife-ills', was the rifle regiment's way of calling us to attention. The RSM would then squeal 'order to arms'. This entailed hefting the rifle up with both hands, catching the trigger guard with two fingers of the right hand, and bringing the left hand down to the left side in two sharp movements. It took a while to get the hang of it and some of the recruits would drop their rifles. 'If it had a bit of hair around it you would soon find it', the RSM would scream. When we were practising for the big T.A. parade in London, RSM MacGregor would start his spiel as he ran up and down the marching ranks. 'Bags of bull men, bags of bull now, and when I give the order "eyes right" I want to hear those fucking eyeballs click.'

I was promoted to Lance Corporal and was a very proud sixteen year old. The parade in London was representative of all the T.A. units in the U.K. and involved standing in Hyde Park for two hours to be reviewed by King George VI and Field Marshall Montgomery. The King and the Field Marshall passed by in a landrover, giving me a view of the sovereign that astonished me. His face was covered in thick pancake makeup. My first thought was this was a doppleganger to protect the King from assassination, but the answer probably lay in the fact that the King had a sick pallor, probably from the effects of cancer from which he was doomed to die some years later.

The Army impressed me with its ability to move big numbers of men around the country, providing hot meals and accommodation all the way from Ulster to London and back. Later on I went on a course for N.C.Os from all units in the 107 Brigade, and passed out with top marks in the final exam. There was another Lance Corporal there from a provincial company of the R.U.R. who spoke with an upper class accent. I think he was a trainee manager or something of the sort. This man was a dozy soldier who turned up with his gaiters on upside down, his uniform unpressed and a very vague attitude to the military arts. I was selected for a commission which pleased me greatly, but when I was dropped in favour of the dozy soldier with the upper class accent, I was very bitter indeed.

My father had always been a Daily Herald reading socialist, and the succession to power of the Labour Party in 1945 had been greeted with celebrations in our house. I can remember still the four inch letters of the Daily Herald in 1945. 'Labour in Power' the headline yelled. We had mock elections at 'Inst'. and I stood as Labour candidate. To everyone's surprise and dismay in that bourgeois establishment, I won. My father saw signs of class discrimination in the reversal of the colonel's decision to give me a commission, and he was probably right. I had imagined that all would be utterly changed with the advent of a Labour Government, and when Manny Shinwell, the veteran socialist of 'Red Clyde' fame became Minister of War, I thought it no contradiction to be a socialist and a member of the T.A. Manny Shinwell actually visited our barracks, had a go on the .22 rifle range, had a word with the Colonel, and left without talking to any of the soldiers, a good few of whom were unemployed. These early experiences left me disillusioned, both with the Labour Party and the army, so I left the T.A. and took a lurch to the left.

However, having been in the T.A., I learnt a lot about life in a group of men where most came from very poor backgrounds. In the army context there was no problem about sectarianism. A good proportion of our battalion's recruits came from poor Catholic ghettos and indeed, all the permanent N.C.Os seemed to be Catholics. The pipe band would play 'The South Down Militia' and 'Kelly The Boy From Killanne' with equal vigour. The army was seen as a British institution with which the Ulster Catholics could identify, whereas the R.U.C. and the auxiliary police were viewed as purely Protestant forces. I have fond memories of the ferocious barking N.C.O.'s who off parade were kindly, patient men who would give ear time to a precocious sixteen year old like myself. 'Good luck to you, R.S.M. "Jigs" MacGregor and Sergeant-Major "Stoker" Lynch, wherever you are!'

About this time, I was reading all the classics, Steinbeck, O'Casey, Jack London's "Iron Heel", plus the Daily Worker which had been delivered to the house through a friend. My father had insisted that the delivery of the paper be cancelled as this could affect his job, and he already had enough problems being a Labour Party supporter. This was the time of Stalin, when communist politics were uncomplicated and the memories of the defence of Leningrad and Stalingrad were still fresh in our minds. Billy MacCullough had polled five thousand votes as a communist party candidate in East Belfast at the 1945 election and the party candidate used to hold rallies in the biggest cinema in Belfast. A whole area of the Albertbridge was known as Stalingrad and I remember the newsreel at the Willowfield cinema showing the victory celebrations for the end of the war in Europe in which all the leaders of the Allies were shown on the screen as the architects of victory. They all got polite applause, including Churchill, but Joe Stalin was cheered to the echo. Belfast in that sense was a European city, in that it followed the leftward swing that came in the wake of World War II when everybody knew that without the sacrifices of the Red Army and the population of the U.S.S.R. we would not have won the war in Europe. These were international and British politics which affected everyone, and the national conflict in Ireland had apparently died with the war. Only in West Belfast was there a Protestant/Catholic divide with Jack Beattie, an anti-partitionist Labour candidate winning with the aid of Protestant Labour votes. The Communist Party at that time recognised partition and indeed was called the Communist Party of Northern Ireland, as the old C.P. of Ireland had dissolved itself for reasons that remain obscure. I suspect that it was a basic nationalist hangover of some of its members who could not bring themselves to support the British war effort, even in support of the Soviet Union.

However, Catholic nationalism in Ireland was considered to have been comprehensively defeated with the Nazis in Germany, whose cause most nationalists in Europe, from the Caucasus to Brittany, had espoused. If there had been no devolved parliament in Northern Ireland at that time, our historic quarrel might have been forgotten. The devolved government in Northern Ireland rubber stamped all the free health and education legislation that ushered in the Welfare State, proving that a local parliament wasn't really necessary and that it was only a slanging cockpit for embittered Catholics and Protestants nursing their hate to keep it warm. Its members really had no purpose other than to extract favours for their constituents and achieve advancement for themselves in a make-believe 'Mickey Mouse' government.

After leaving the T.A. I wasted my spare time for about a year going to dances and drinking in the pubs in Newcastle at the weekends. Sometimes I used to visit a pub on the Donegall Quay in Belfast, called the Anchor Bar, which had a Saturday night sing-song. Behind the main bar was a room with wooden benches and tables and a platform at the top end. It reminded me of a school room, with no decoration except a mirror advertisement for Comber Whiskey. At that time Guinness marketed a stout called Single X or porter, which was half the strength of bottled stout, but was sold from the barrel in pints. Rows of mainly middle-aged and older working men sat at the forms while the waiter dispensed pints of porter from a double decked tray with holes in the top deck for the pint tumblers. The M.C. would go to the platform and announce from a piece of paper that John or Sammy was requested to sing his 'pleasure'. The singer, whose name would have been submitted by a friend, would go to the platform with a show of reluctance and deliver his party piece. The songs were mostly old music hall songs like 'The Boers have got my daddy, my soldier dad', or the odd industrial ballad like 'Ballynure Green'

> 'There's weavers and winders in aprons of white
> Some work by day and some work by the night
> But there's one wee lassie and she is their Queen
> And she works in John Ross's in Ballynure Green'.

The singer, no matter how incompetent his rendering, got a hearing and fulsome praise from the chairman when he finished. I say 'he' because no women would be there. This, in the days when women were invading the new lounge bars, was a bastion of male exclusivity. Remembering now, as I write, I wish I had copied down some of the songs, as some of them I have never heard again, even though I was actively involved in the folk revival of the sixties.

Finding life in an office a slow death, with a pittance of £3.50 a week at the age of eighteen, I started casting around for another job. The jobs that I applied for were mostly sales related, but if I got as far as an interview, there were interviewees in dozens queueing up the stairs. The reality of unemployment, the greatest curse in our province from which a lot of our other problems spring, was brought home to me in this period. Eventually I decided to study for some qualification which would give me a passport to escape from the ranks of the unskilled. My pal was a cook in the Merchant Navy, a big tradition in Belfast, which had boasted its own shipping line, and of course had, in Harland and Wolff, the biggest shipyard in the world at that time. I decided to enroll in night classes at the Marine Radio College for the Post Masters' Certificate in radio-telegraphy, which would qualify me as a radio officer in the Merchant Navy. Four nights a week I would journey from East Belfast to South Belfast to receive lectures in radio theory, electricity and magnetism, morse code and commercial working and fault finding in marine radio equipment. I had to pay my own fees of eight pounds a quarter, which was hard going on £3.50 a week. Wireless operating, I discovered, was a lot more complicated than most people thought, requiring one to understand the working and mathematics of all components used. eg. valves, resisters, coils, capacitators etc. It took two long years, sometimes causing me despair when my morse speeds would slip back, or when 80% of the pupils would fail their examination, as often happened. Some failed their morse test through nervousness and were able to resit in three months' time, and to achieve this was the most I could hope. Whenever I sat the examination, content in the knowledge that I had studied hard, I was not really surprised when the fat envelope with the gold embossed 'ticket' plopped on the mat. This modest success gave me new self confidence and pleased my parents, who thought I had frittered away my time at school.

My mother was dying of cancer at the time, so I stayed at home to share her last months. It is a cruel thing that such a talented woman was cut down at the early age of forty-seven, with such an unremitting disease. Forty years on, it is still scything through the population with, more or less, the same ineffectual treatments. Man has been to the moon and back, missiles can laser into windows of buildings hundreds of miles away, yet this fundamental problem of health and life remains unsolved.

I received promotion in work and now was a sales representative with a good salary and a free car for extolling the virtues of Stork Margarine around the shops of Ulster. This meant that I would lose money by going to sea, but I am glad to say that I had the good sense to leave and join the Marconi Company at £24 a month.

My mother spent one year racked by pain, withered away and eventually died, weighing about three stone. In her life she had developed herself to the utmost, specially in the theatre. She had been a former member of the semi-professional Arts Theatre which brought to the stage in Belfast for the first time plays by Beckett, Tennessee Williams, Anouihl and Arthur Koestler etc. Actors like Jimmy Ellis of 'Z Cars' fame and Patrick Magee graduated from this theatre, and she also produced the first play in which Belfast's inimitable James Young first appeared. This was Jack Loudan's 'Story for Today' where Jimmy played a comic part in what was otherwise a serious play. He completely stole the show and the play was performed all over Northern Ireland as word spread about this marvellous comic actor.

During my mother's illness only James Young came often to see her and dispelled the gloom with his spontaneous bubbling humour. He went far in his profession, knew and loved his Belfast, and was a caring and thoughtful human being, now also sadly missed.

My brother had been brought home from Egypt where he was serving with a Field Security section of the Intelligence Corps. He was transferred to Thiepval Barracks, Lisburn and lived at home. Shortly after my mother's death he contracted T.B. complicated by diabetes, and was discharged from the Army. Nature had given him a raw deal and he lived out the rest of his life as a semi-invalid. Mother died in March and I immediately gave in my notice and prepared to go to sea. I set about buying my uniforms with elation mixed with a certain apprehension.

A LEAP IN THE DARK

Reporting to the Marconi Office in Liverpool I was told to go to the waiting room where Radio Officers from ships docking in the port made their reports. I had booked into the 'Flying Angel Club', which is a seamen's hostel run by the Church of England, there to find a new world of mates, engineers, "paying offs" and "signings on". A bald middle-aged man from Eire was getting ready to go to the Indian Coast where he would be for two years. Another fellow, an Englishman, had been paid off a Head Line ship, which was obviously not to his liking, remarking that it had white officers and a Belfast crew. Later in my career I would have given my eye teeth to sail with a Belfast crew and to enjoy the rich humour and banter that is unique to my native city.

Yet another was from Co. Down but lived in England, had not been home for some years and wanted to know all about the changes in Hillsborough. The Marconi clerk sent for me. I signed some papers and was told to join the M.V. Port Napier in the Gladstone dock. Liverpool was then a bustling place with an overhead railway, miles of docks with crowded streets where the seamen of every nationality jostled among the 'scousers'. I found the Gladstone dock and went aboard the Port Napier in the mixture of excitement and trepidation of one who is about to embark on a new life.

The Port Line, now defunct, ran refrigerated cargo ships to Australia and New Zealand and each of its ships carried some twelve passengers as well. The Port Napier was spotless, wooden decks scrubbed white, and paintwork perfect. I found 'Sparkie', as the sailors called the chief Radio Officer, and presented myself as the new trainee. He had been on this run to New Zealand for twelve years, was very set in his ways and I thought him a mousy nondescript little man with a Lancashire accent, and not very welcoming. I was shown my cabin which was very small but comfortable enough. A strong smell of diesel fuel permeated the ship. The clanking of winches, the cursing of dockers, sailors and stewards bustling hither and yon, completed the strange atmosphere in which I found myself.

In those days the Merchant Navy was still regarded as a service, and indeed if it came to war, we would have been conscripted. Part of this ethos was the rank structure which I had not thought much about. The deck and engineering departments were, as they say, oil and water, and they didn't mix. The 'sparkies', as we were called, were somewhere in between, more close to the deck, but regarded as 'Johnny-come-latelies'. I found myself in the saloon, seated with the white tabbed deck apprentices who resented my single, wavy gold bar of rank. They were young, ex-public school boys who, of course, had years of sea experience and I was soon to find that my shore job and two years of radio school did not impress them. However, it was ever thus, the new boy has to make his bed and lie in it. Their attitudes were very snobbish and chauvinist and they really did believe they had won a prize in the lottery of life, in that they had been born English gentlemen and, as such, were unwilling to examine any other cultures.

Their greatest contempt was for the engineers who spoke with strong, regional accents and lived in a world of oil, grease and thunderous noise. Most of the engineers at that time had completed a five year apprenticeship in a shipyard and were quite at home in this environment. The deck officers resented them having officer rank without knowing, as it were, the blunt end of the ship from the sharp end. Life has taught me that each skill is uniquely precious and that a man who masters his craft supremely is worthy of respect. Those public school boys would have yet to learn that in the wider life outside the realms of ships and seafaring, the art of ship husbandry and navigation was not uppermost in people's thoughts. There is the story of the ship's master, vaguely listening to a conversation on the subject of comic opera around the saloon table, who asked his officers: 'Gilbert and Sullivan? Where does that company run to?'

The atmosphere of a ship preparing for sea is like nothing else on Earth, except perhaps an Army unit marching out of barracks after a two year tour of duty. Everything that will be needed has to be ordered, checked, and then stowed away. Ten miles out at sea is too late to remember something essential. The result of this is a bustling of chief officers, chief stewards and chief engineers, all running about with clipboards and invoices, piles of pipes and flanges, tablecloths and crockery, paint and chemicals being checked and shouted over. Then, having signed ship's articles in the presence of the captain, we made ready to sail. The Port Napier was, I was told, sailing 'light ship' which meant nothing to me then, but later as the ship lurched and wallowed through the mountainous Irish Sea, I vowed never to set foot on a light ship again. The bow would rise up to the crest of a thirty foot wave and then plunge down into the trough. This would cause the stern to rise out of the water sending great shudders of vibration through the ship which threatened to sunder it, plate from plate. Before the ship's bow surfaced from the tons of foamy white water to face the next roller, she would give a sideways roll causing the eardrums to swirl and leaving the body without a sense of balance. My stomach heaved and churned while I tried to make sense of the dots and dashes that came through the earphones. My chair would slide from one end of the radio room to the other, the ship would give an unexpected sideways lurch, green bile would fill my mouth and I would rush for the rails to evacuate my stomach. The others were suffering equally, the poor engineers also having to endure the heat and noise of the engine room. I never managed to distinguish one radio station from another in these conditions, as in the Irish Sea hundreds of ships over a hundred mile radius were all transmitting 'GLV DE GBSO QRU?' which meant 'Seaforth radio being called by British ship, call sign GBSO, have you any telegrams for me?' 'CQ DE GLD TFC LIST UP512'. This meant that Lands End radio would broadcast a list of ships for which they had telegrams on 512 kilocycles. It is all very confusing but when one is green from sea sickness it is impossible. We headed out past Lands End and into the North Atlantic. Still the gale raged. Sea sickness is a source of great mirth for some people, like old sailors who have little else about which to feel superior, stand up comics and the like, but in all truth it is a debilitating and awful sickness which is not even relieved by the act of vomiting . After three days I contemplated suicide but rejected it on the grounds that drowning would be even more stressful. Ten days elapsed before the storm abated as we sailed into the calm waters of the Caribbean. What transpired in those last seven days I don't remember.

    My boss, Mr. Hargreaves, having thirty years sea service, seemed to have little interest in life other than his home, his wife and his berth on the Port Napier which afforded him a fortnight's leave every three months. When it is considered that in the British Merchant Navy of those days one could be away from home for two years if the ship did not visit a home port, I suppose a ship on a regular run was not to be sneezed at. The four weeks we were in New Zealand, Mr Hargreaves did not go ashore once. Yet he had led an interesting life. He had served on the Arctic convoys and had had a shell pass through the radio room during a naval battle. He could type long telegrams and weather reports direct from morse which I never mastered.

At heart here was a plain Lancashire man, neat and methodical in his habits who should have been in an insurance office or the civil service but, like so many, having learned the trick of surviving one milieu, was frightened to take the plunge into another one. We sailed to the Dutch island of Curacao, not to Willenstadt, the capital, but to an oil berth which contained only a pier and a control shack beside a long sandy beach. The junior electrician, also a first tripper, darted ashore as soon as the gangway was down, in spite of an imprecation written in chalk on a blackboard that there was no shore leave. The first mate caught him red-handed coming up the gang plank five minutes before we were due to sail. His freckles and red hair that seemed to resist all attempts to control, topping his white tunic and slacks, made him an incongruous figure. 'What did you expect to find ashore anyway?' bellowed the mate surveying the blank expanse of sand. 'Thought there would be native girls,' said the electrician in his mangled Geordie vowels. Next stop was Cristobal, the city at the entrance to the Panama Canal. The multitude of ships, the palm lined quays, the myriad varieties of the human race from all the continents and the excited sounds of Spanish seemed to make the years of study, the misery of seasickness and the closed society all worthwhile. Panama, 'How shall I describe it? Now the hub of the universe', as the poet Keats described it: 'Silent like stout Cortez, Looking when with eagle's eyes he stared at the Pacific, All his men looked at each other, with a wild surmise, Silent upon a peak in Darien'. A home to the Matan Indians, colonised by the Spaniards who brought their language, architecture and religion. Its jungle covered hills presented the shortest barrier between the Atlantic and Pacific. The growing economy of California in the last century and the difficulties of the long journey through the Rockies by expensive rail transport or round the Magellan Straits made it cost effective to drive a waterway through the Isthmus. The sea level difference between the Atlantic and the Pacific made it necessary to have a two way series of locks where the ships were hauled by powerful electric locomotives, called mules, to the next level. In all, I think I must have sailed through the Canal about twelve times, and each time has been a source of excitement and wonder.

About a hundred ships of all shapes and sizes were moored in the lake outside the Canal so we were afforded a night ashore while the backlog was cleared. I went ashore by myself, in streets teeming with colour and life. The varieties of race were amazing, pure gold skinned Indians, mulattos of every shade. Greeks, Spaniards and Chinese mingled in the streets and bars. I was importuned into a nightclub by an attractive girl who disappeared as soon as I paid my entrance money. There followed a floorshow which was wholly erotic and performed with gusto. One coffee coloured lady completed her dancing act by wrapping herself round a pillar and grinding away with abandon. Later in life I was to learn that such erotic acts are a fraud and can only work due to the fevered imagination of the voyeurs.

On then through the Canal to New Zealand, three whole weeks away without a sight of land or ship. I took over the night watch which was surplus to requirements on such a small ship, but gave me an opportunity to learn my job without disrupting radio traffic. In this way I could take my time in the dead of night to ask for repeats, etc. The Port Napier was a weather reporting ship which meant that weather conditions were transmitted to the meterological service in Britain every six hours. At night time conditions are better for transmission distances so it was possible to raise Portishead radio directly without routing the telegrams through the then existing Commonwealth relay system via Vancouver, Singapore or Cape Town radios. Some operators' morse was rhythmic and steady, while others went for speed, using bug keys which operated sideways, one side sending a stream of dots and the other side sending a series of dashes, depending on the length of time the key was depressed. This, however, achieved little in communication efficiency as an atmospheric crackle or fading of signal strength rendered the copy unintelligible, leading to requests for repeats.

By the time we reached New Zealand I had got the hang of it, now taking a pride in transmitting and receiving important messages for the ship. There came with this competence a new sense of self-esteem, with the knowledge that the mates, sailors, engineers and stewards could depend on me for a link with the outside world.

The Port Napier throbbed through the Pacific, flying fish flitting across the deck at night, undulating schools of porpoises stretching as far as the eye could see at daylight. This magnificent sight would greet me as I came off watch at dawn. The porpoises swam in unison with a certain rhythm, like synchronised swimmers in a Hollywood musical. They seemed drawn by curiosity and they would follow the ship for days at a time. Those golden Pacific dawns, with the porpoises for company, stamped an image on my mind that lingers still.

Early one beautiful Pacific morning I had a few minutes to spare before going down to breakfast, when the receiver picked up a voice with a strong Australian/New Zealand accent, exorting potential punters to examine the merits of a second-hand pram for sale on the Karangahappi Road in Auckland. This was New Zealand Commercial Radio coming within the ship's range and was a foretaste of the terrible parochialism which I was to find in that rich, beautiful, but boring, country.

I woke up the next morning in the beautiful bay of Auckland, the city grew closer, and eventually we tied up at one of the fingers of concrete that poked out from the city into the bay. Devonport, the suitably named home of the Royal New Zealand Navy, lay over to the east of the harbour, with three sleek grey destroyers lying in an indolent row in stark contrast to the bustle of the commercial harbour. Ropes secured, then letters arrived and 'wharfies,' as the Kiwi dockers are called, swarmed all over the ship. A telephone was installed and Paddy Hurley, one of our Irish quartermasters, took up his position as our gangway watchman. Impatient as I ever was I dashed ashore, still in uniform, to see New Zealand. Auckland in those days had few buildings over two stories and the bar I went into had walls of white tiles like a public urinal. It was still early in the morning and there were quite a few dockers in shorts and sweatshirts lining the circular central bar. The barman was dispensing glasses of beer called 'schooners' from hose and nozzle like a petrol pump. A schooner cost sixpence and there was nothing else available.

This was an unpromising start but I returned to the ship determined not to be deterred by first impressions, to make use of my time (and I would have plenty of it) to learn about the life and culture of this, the farthest English speaking country from my own. In those days in the fifties in which air travel was restricted and expensive, none of my acquaintances could have hoped to visit as far afield as the Antipodies. Indeed most emigrants had to take the chance of going there sight unseen and unfortunately many lived to regret it.

DOUBLE LOCKAGE, PEDRO MIGUEL, PANAMA CANAL

AUCKLAND BAY, NEW ZEALAND

KIWI CAPERS

Berthed behind us was a Norwegian ship unloading phosphates from the island of Nauru of which I was to hear more in later years, but apart from that there was little of interest going on in the harbour itself. The city of Auckland was in a beautiful setting, gently sloping hills covered with foliage giving way to wooden bungalows and then concrete urban landscape to the shore. As everywhere, the people are more interesting than the landscape and the wharfies were as foulmouthed as any I have heard but the pinched New Zealand accent rendered the copious 'fucks and blinds' merely incongruous.

However they were a cheerful lot, stripped to the waist in bright tropical sunshine, they bantered their workmates unmercifully as they swung the carcasses of frozen lambs on board. They were very well organised and had breaks for what they called 'Smoko' which they took in their modern canteen. It is said that they once went on strike due to the failure of management to provide straws for their free milk. New Zealand was partly settled by early trade unionists fleeing the oppression and blacklists of nineteenth century Britain and the Labour Party had been in power there for over a decade The Communist Party of New Zealand had a strong industrial base and owned the only decent bookshop in Auckland. It later became the main ally of Albania and indeed was responsible for much of Albania's foreign policy towards the English speaking world.

The CPNZ controlled the wharfies union and I must say they obtained excellent wages and conditions for their members. When there were shortages for the loading gangs, the stevadores would take on members of ships crews who were free to work, and as the radio room was closed down I was always available for work when it came. A full day's work in the freezer hold brought £5-£6, when my salary from Marconi brought £6 a week, so the work was very welcome. There were four gangs in the hold and when the sling of lamb carcasses came down, each gang took its turn to stow them away. You usually had to wait about five minutes for your next sling to arrive so all in all, it was easy work for a young, fit man. The regular wharfies included two Maoris and a Hungarian and there was much racial and sexual banter at their expense. Apparently, traditionally the Maoris went into battle with full erections, so much was made of this, and a fine sight it must have made. The Maoris however gave as good as they got and there seemed to be no malice involved. The rest of the crew were engaged in maintainance work but I found myself with a lot of free time and indeed money, but there seemed to be little on which I could spend it. As walking was always my joy, I used to take the tram to the end of the lines and tramp through the hills that ringed the city or sometimes I would hitch-hike to the beaches out to the east. The Auckland Hills sustained fine fruit orchards managed by Croatians, referred to as 'Dallies', i.e. from Dalmatia, who must have established an emigration pattern early on and taken advantage of the similar climate and cheap land to grow what they were used to growing at home. In later years I spent happy holidays on the Dalmation coast and met the 'Dallies' home on holidays from New Zealand with the New Zealand flag proudly displayed in the windows of their cars. Life in New Zealand may be pleasant and rewarding, while life on a peasant holding in Yugoslavia is undoubtably hard, but there is a vibrant atmosphere in the villages of the coastal Yugoslavia which those emigrants must miss.

Walking alone among the cherry blossoms and palms of the Auckland hills I chanced upon a typical wooden bungalow surounded by bougainvillaea. The name plate said 'Donaghadee,' the name of a coastal village near Belfast. It threw me into a paroxysm of homesickness. This is an odd feeling, one feels a definite physical pain, an acute longing for sights and sounds familiar, which there is no assuaging. I longed to call and introduce myself but my nerve failed me, so I tramped on, wishing I was at home at the other side of the world. This homesickness eventually passed but I think it is a factor which must be considered when deciding to go abroad for good.

The Orange Hall in Ulster rural life is a focus for social activity for Protestant people, so it was rather surprising to find that there was an Orange Hall in Auckland which served the same purpose, only in this case the Protestant exclusivity was not so evident. The dance that was held there probably was the biggest in Auckland and the patrons danced 'The Pride of Erin', the 'Valeeta', and other old time dances which their ancestors brought from Ireland and Scotland in the last century. At the interval all hands retired to the basement where cocoa and buns were to be had at refectory tables. I sat down beside a blonde girl and a man who had been in the New Zealand Navy in the war. He told me he had been off the Normandy coast at 'D' Day and had swum ashore and back again just to say he had been in France. I think that says something about the isolation of New Zealand at that time. This man, who was an affable enough working class New Zealander, then passed a perjorative remark about the Maoris. The blond girl then announced that she was part Maori, causing much embarrassment all round. I learned later that 25% of New Zealand's population had Maori blood. I observed that the Maoris, who were a fine looking people in general, had a great enthusiasm for, and a very low tolerance of, alcohol, swilling down schooners of beer as if their guts were on fire. In part this was due to the six o'clock closing which was in force at the time, forcing people to drink as much as they could before six. Known as the 'five o'clock swill', the pubs would fill up with thirsty workers and at about five thirty the Maoris would start sliding to the floor and were sometimes even sick. I could see the sense of the tiled walls when the barmen hosed down the premises at closing time. Carry-outs were ordered in cases and barrels and groups of men would head home to finish their carousals. For the seamen there was nothing else for it but to head back to the ship for the night. At the dance at the Orange Hall later on in the evening there would be a body search for illicit booze on entering, but the ingenious Kiwis could be seen burying their bottles under the bushes in the grounds, to be redeemed later with the aid of a passout. This was the Ulster heritage in New Zealand, Aughnacloy in the Antipodes, joy in industry and sobriety in pleasure, that is if it couldn't be helped.

    A visiting sailor's view of a land is necessarily a superficial one but I had the impression of a land of milk and honey, with full employment at high wages, free healthcare and education, with a class conscious working class who achieved all these benefits back in the thirties, long before anywhere in Europe. But oh, the boredom, the long close-down at the weekends when the streets resembled Ballymena on a wet Sunday. The paucity of intellectual or cultural life which sends most of its gifted people abroad, which gives an atmosphere of isolation, gave me a depression which could only be shaken off by the thought that I did not have to stay, whereas many thousands of immigrants, having made their bed, had to lie in it. The wages there were three times what could be earned in the U.K. and indeed my job on a New Zealand coaster paid five times as well. Yet we had New Zealanders on our ship working as stewards and firemen for the sake of getting away for a while.

There were no apparent prostitutes in New Zealand, the coarse seamen observing that there was too much amateur competition. The telephone was ringing at all times with calls for the company of the ship's officers or crew at private parties. The Maories practised a courtship pattern which involved bringing the boy friend home to meet the parents and then to bed. A great culture shock to an Ulsterman to be sure but the European New Zealanders seemed to think the last part was worth emulating. We left Auckland after three weeks and sailed down past the jungled Coramandel Penninsula to Port Lyttleton in South Island. Port Lyttleton consisted of five piers, a railway line, some wooden houses and a magnificent back drop of mountains. Life there was as exciting as watching paint dry. The pubs closed at six o'clock so the sailors didn't have anywhere at all to go at night. I took a day out to Christ Church, the capital of South Island, on a wild west railway with wooden carriages and running boards, only to find a sleepy wooden town which somebody compared to a graveyard with traffic lights. All in all I was quite excited when the time came to leave New Zealand and fall in again with the ship's work routine at sea. The Port Napier, holds packed with frozen lamb, headed into the blue calm Pacific, back through the ever wondrous Panama Canal, and thence to the crowded docks of East London.

HOME FROM THE SEA

King George V Docks in London were part of a huge complex of dockland that ran for many miles along the north bank of the Thames from London Bridge to Tilbury in Essex. They were crowded at that time with mainly British passenger/cargo ships, Shaw Saville, Port Line, P & O, Blue Funnel and others with established routes to Australasia and the Far East.

The London docks at that time must have employed twenty thousand dockers and the communities round about were rich in pub life, good value fish and chip shops, barrow boys with humourous cockney patter and everywhere the landscape dominated by the funnels and masts of the ocean leviathans. As I write, I read how they are being made over into high rent bourgeois ghettoes where water skiers play where thousands once laboured.

A Port Line shore crew came aboard and those who had been thrown together for three months to live cheek by jowl were dispersed without sentiment or formality. Being on a ship is like being in prison as Dr. Johnston once said, and as in prison you get to know everything about your companions, but then when the voyage is completed you go your separate ways, probably never to meet again. Friendships are rarely forged by just common work, but experiences shared on board ship do form a bond of sorts, and I have always been pleased to meet former shipmates again.

Back in Belfast my brother had been discharged from the army with diabeties and T.B. and lay in Forster Green hospital for what at that time was a two year cure, if any. Luckily the B.G.C. vaccine had arrived and he was cured in nine months of the T.B. but his army career was finished and he had no training for anything else. This first homecoming as a merchant seaman was for me the glorious highpoint of my youth. In those days when foreign travel was the perogative of the rich, foreign travel meant emigration and was indeed a sad affair, so to be able to speak with authority of strange lands and seas at the age of twenty-two, was indeed an achievement.

At that time my youth hostelling friends met for a pint at the Duke of York pub which was a pleasant hostelry frequented by newspapermen and shipyard intellectuals. Later it was to be famous, or infamous, as the place of work of one Gerry Adams, reputed to be 'terrorist in chief' in

Northern Ireland. Later we would adjourn to the Ulster Milk Bar where topers and theatre goers would meet and talk. The evening would finish up with us standing at the door watching the homeward bound citizens and putting the world to rights. Those who lived over the bridge would pause again at the junction of the Beersbridge and Castlereagh Roads and further discuss the past, present and future of humanity. Friendships of youth are intense and fulfilling where we divulge our hopes and ambitions, little knowing that these bright hopeful years are the hopeful travelling, which is inevitably better than arrival.

ON MY OWN

With the fortnight's leave over all too soon, the telegram from Marconi arrived with orders to report to Marconi depot in East Ham. The depot waiting room for R.O.'s was the only place where it was possible to discuss the world of marine wireless with fellow operators in person. Union branches held meetings which were non-events due to the membership being at sea most of the time and the difficulty of finding a quorum. I discovered we were being exploited by Marconi who charged the shipping company the maximum rate of pay for our services and, as it took twelve years' service to reach maximum pay, the difference was in the pocket of Marconi. We also had to take any ship to which we were assigned, with the possibility of being away for two years at a time.

My assignment was to the S.S. Ravenspoint at Shadwell Basin in Wapping where I arrived to find an elderly, rusting coal burning coaster of 3,000 tons with a woodbine funnel and a straight bow. The dock contained a sludge of muddy oily water surrounded by scabrous, crumbling warehouses built in the last century. The toilets on the dock were labelled bluntly 'Whites' and 'Asiatics' although this owed more to the toilet customs of the two races than apartheid.

The Ravenspoint belonged to the MacAndrew Lines, traded to Portugal and Spain, and was a relic of the fast disappearing steam age. The radio room and R.O's cabin were added on as an afterthought and were perched on the deck between the bridge and the lifeboats. The cabin, finished with tongue and groove walls, had enough room only to stand up and dress, otherwise one had to sit on the bunk. The tiny saloon had two tables for eight officers, varnished oak walls adorned with a photograph of the Queen and set off with brass fittings and portholes. The shuffling Arab firemen completed the atmosphere of Conrad's river steamer. The whole ship was black from coal dust from the bunkers which were being loaded, so I got out of my expensive doeskin uniform fast. I was told later that my appearance in full rig was a source of great hilarity amongst the crew. I met the chief mate, an elderly Scot whose first question was 'How long have you been afloat son?' His fat ruddy face was topped by a panama hat with a hole through which a lock of grey hair protruded. He had served his time in Windjammers round the Horn and had been at sea ever since.

I came to realise that he had been so long at sea that he had lost all contact with shore life and referred to all manner of things in nautical terms. 'The decentest man afloat' he would describe an aquaintance he admired. A toilet would be blocked with 'A fathom of shite.' The man stayed on board all the time, as the ship was the only home he knew. Later, when we were due to get a new captain, he came to the radio room to find out how the direction finder worked, as we had no radar and relied on the direction finder to navigate up the English channel in foggy weather. I explained how we obtained cross bearings from both the English and French coasts thus giving a fairly true ship's position. He stared silently at the D.F. console for a while and then uttered the expression of utter bafflement 'The cunning buggers, the cunning buggers'. He padded back to his cabin still muttering 'The cunning buggers'. I suppose he felt the same bafflement about radio navigation as my generation feels about computers today. The captain, known as 'Jack the Ripper' to the cockney sailors, was a wiry wee Orkney islander in his forties. The Orkneys, without enough land to support the population, spawn seamen like Ballymacarrett spawns shipyardmen, and this captain knew his trade backwards and had the height of contempt for the cockney sailors who he reckoned were only at sea to dodge National Service. The second mate had been a fighter pilot during the war and sported a handle-bar moustache. He was an intelligent, well educated man in his late twenties, who never talked about his background and later left the company to do a two year contract with British-India, a contract most officers would avoid like the plague. The third engineer was a cheerful Ceylonese of Portuguese ancestry who often referred to 'wogs' and 'coons' but whose black irises and sallow complexion indicated a fair measure of coloured blood in himself. It is sad when people embrace the dominant culture to the extent of denying their own ancestry.

The radio room on the S.S. Ravenspoint boasted one medium wave transmitter, one receiver and a direction finder. There was also the standard auto alarm which was activated by twelve dashes sent on 500 kcs. As we were never more than 300 miles from the coast it was not thought necessary to have short wave transmission. The clanking of winches and the curses of the dockers finally subsided, a pilot came aboard and we nosed out of the Shadwell Basin into the Thames. If I hadn't felt so apprehensive it would have been a marvellous pleasure cruise, seeing London without the bustle and noise of the underground.

I stood on the deck and watched the boroughs of East and South London glide by until we dropped the pilot at Greenwich. Once outside the port limits it was my duty to send a notification of our ship's leaving of Port of London and our port of destination, in this case Lisbon. I started the transmitter generator and with trembling fingers and thumb, grasped the morse key. I thought of all the embarrassment if I disrupted the communications of the whole English channel. But two years of practice steadied my nerve and I sent the signal GNI de GBSP TGR up 512. This meant Niton radio being called by British ship Ravenspoint for a traffic report, listen out on the working frequency of 512 kcs. As well as the morse code there is a radio shorthand which one only learns at sea. Wx is for weather, O.M. is for 'old man' or the captain while the ubiquitous O.K. comes from the Greek Olle Kalo which the Greek operators used as the affirmative. 'Niton radio' replied straight away 'GBSPde GNI R' meaning message received, retune to 512 kcs. 5oo kcs is the international calling frequency and in the English channel it is a cacophany of hundreds of ships calling English, French, Belgian and Dutch coast stations. The working frequency of 512 kcs is relatively quiet and there the signal was: 'GBSP2 de G.N.I. hw?' (How are you receiving me?); 'G.N.I de GBSP R ere T.R'. (Hearing you loud and clear. Here is my traffic report); S.S. Ravenspoint leaving London and bound Lisbon.

This procedure over, I sat down to keep my first watch. The jangle of morse rang in my ears, gradually lifting me out of a world of one ship into an imaginary world of Polish ships heading for the Baltic ports from China and French ships homing into Brest from Guadaloupe. The well known British liners like the Queen Mary spat out their TR's as they approached Southhampton water. Unlike the rest of the crew, the R.O. works two hours on and two hours off, but often is required to work right through his off watch period if the radio traffic requires it. At ten pm. I finished my last watch for the day, signed off the log, set the auto alarm and returned from the world of morse code and imagination to the confines of the ship. The stand-by sailor brought the third mate and myself a cup of cocoa which no doubt was the correct soporific for one going to bed, but hardly the correct beverage for the officer of the watch who is supposed to keep his eyes skinned for other ships to avoid collisions. However, it was ever thus in the Merchant Navy, cocoa on the bridge at night.

Three o'clock in the morning, a rap on the cabin door: 'The old man wants you to take a radio bearing, Sparks'. The cockney stand-by sailor seemed happy in his work, waking me up. As I had only performed the function theoretically in the Radio College, I set about the task with trepidation. A fog had descended in the channel and the captain had only a vague idea where we were by dead reckoning, and needed an accurate position. I found a British radio beacon coming in loud and clear on the receiver. The goniometer was then twisted to an area of zero sound which meant that the D.F. loop was at right angles to the incoming signal. Reading the number off the scale I shouted this through the voice tube to the bridge, also the time. Then the same thing was done with a French radio beacon. The angles were marked off on the chart and where the two lines crossed was the position of the ship. The same procedure was followed every hour leaving a series of crosses which marked our progress down the English Channel. Radar at that time was just being introduced to Merchant shipping but the navigators were coming to rely on it too much. Nowadays there is decca navigation which is read off a computer and satellite navigation where a fix can be had at any time if the shipping company pays the fee. On the old radars a ship could be obscured on the screen by a lot of clutter or 'snow' with the navigator thinking the way ahead was clear.

Two mornings later I was awakened by an enormous thud. As if in a nightmare, my eyes unbelievingly watched the door frame reshape itself into a diamond shape and back again to normal. A long crunching sound of metal rubbing on metal followed. The ship's hooter sounded, so now wide awake and frightened I leapt out of bed and pulled on my trousers. I started the transmitter generator with one hand and pulled out my life jacket with the other. The porthole darkened with a moving black cover. Rushing up on deck I saw a huge wall of steel, many times the size of our little ship, pull away from our side. The huge tanker's screw, half out of the water, churned white water slowly. The name on the tanker's stern was French and it's port of registry was Brest. Below me on the lower deck our twenty stone cockney cook was leaning over the rail shouting 'Any Geordies on board?' Gallows humour I thought as I didn't know if we were sinking or not. I noticed the radar scanner turning away on the monkey island far above our little toy of a ship. With a collision of such force I felt surely we must be sinking so, without waiting for orders from the bridge, I turned on the generator and as soon as the valves were heated I sent out the international signal S.O.S.

S.O.S. S.O.S. 'British ship Ravenspoint in collision with French tanker—'. Then I realised that this was meaningless without a position so, in a panic, I blew through the communication tube to the bridge and asked where we were. 'Off Cape Finistere', the voice on the bridge answered. Composing myself I returned to the morse key and completed the message. This of course was the wrong thing to do as a distress signal should only be sent where there is a danger to the ship, which apparently wasn't the case. Luckily I had not sent the twelve dashes to activate the auto-alarms of ships whose R.O's were off watch. Then in slow, measured, rhythmic morse the French tanker's operator came over the ether. 'GBSP DE FNRC'. 'French ship Belleville. Are you badly damaged?' The answer to this of course I didn't know so I decided to draw a veil over my S.O.S. transmission, hoping that it had gone unheard. On the other hand, I had had to take a split second decision and judged that there would be no time for investigations. It turned out that the ship's rail had been bent and some plates above the water line had been buckled. The French tanker was sailing without cargo and was so high in the water that his radar beams didn't pick us up. Details of the ship's owners and destinations were exchanged and we sailed on past Vigo to the Portuguese coast. Thirty-five years later, my wife and I were travelling back from a camping trip in Germany when the Zeebrugge Ferry seemed to be aground. I instinctively knew that it was not safe, though the Belgian steward smiled at my anxiety. 'It was only a sandbank', he said, 'no need to worry, it happens all the time'. Three months later, the water-logged Herald of Free Enterprise turned over on its side on that same sandbank with considerable loss of life. The moral is that at sea one cannot be too careful.

    The good old Ravenspoint, with it's rivetted plates and woodbine funnel sailed proudly into the Tagus Estuary the next day, past one of the most magnificent landfalls in the world. A series of mediaeval forts, complete with castelated walls and cannons, marked our progress into Lisbon. A pilot launch with a party of quaintly named 'Financial Police' came aboard. Their uniforms were pure Ruritanian, grey linen tunics with old fashioned high necks, jodhpurs and riding boots topped off by high kepis in blue and green. What their function was, was a mystery, but emigration officers came aboard when we docked, looked at the crew list and barred two members of the crew from going ashore. The reason for this was that Poland was a communist country although the two Poles we had refused to go back to Poland after the war, and were more anti-communist than the Pope.

Portugal then was a fascist country governed by an aging Professor of Economics called Salazar. All political activity was forbidden, trade unions were banned and the Catholic church wrote the rule book of human behaviour. Lisbon to me was, and is, the most beautiful city in Europe, with its mosaic patterned streets, majestic squares, pavement cafes and cheerful people. My first trip ashore was past the Financial Policeman on the gangplank, on to an open tram where the conductor swung along the running board to collect the fares and so to the city centre. Seafaring men tend to go ashore alone and then team up with whoever happens along at the time and, in that haphazard way, where one ends up is in the lap of the gods.

SS RAVENPOINT, APPROACHING LISBON

LISBON NIGHTS

As it happened, most of the crew of the Ravenspoint who had been running to Lisbon for five years had a very established pattern of behaviour. First stop was the Brittania Bar where pints of beer could be had for the equivalent of six old pence. The Brittania was dark, dusty and entirely given over to the unimpeded consumption of alcohol. Brandies, wine and beer appeared on the greasy varnished counter or to be taken to the round brown tables. There were no embellishments in the Brittannia whatsoever. The dun brown walls were enlivened only by a fly-blown advertisement for Watney's beer. Portuguese bank clerks, shopkeepers and tradesmen rubbed shoulders with cockney sailors, oblivious of the gloomy surroundings, quaffing pint after brandy, silently, before departing for the train station across the road to catch the train home to Cascais or Estoril. It is still there, the same serious and sombre cavern I knew as a youth, innocent of fresh paint as it was then but alas the cockney sailors are no more, as the British Merchant Navy is no more, sacrificed by that super patriot Margaret Thatcher to the God of Mammon, wrapped up in a 'Mickey Mouse' flag of convenience. Anyway, our sailors would stay long enough to get up a head of steam and then on to the Texas bar, which was a different kettle of fish altogether. The Texas bar had a flyover street above it and had the impression of being an underground tunnel. It was, and still is, a gathering place of prostitutes and sailors, devoid of any attempt at social intercourse. Drinks are drunk and paid for, the business with the ladies is transacted, whereupon the clients depart with the girls to the hotel around the corner for the deal to be completed. It was a favourite spot for seamen from short stay ships such as tankers or passenger ships where the crew can only get ashore for a few hours before sailing. A dismal and depressing house to be sure, but I suppose it has a function in the great scheme of things.

The Atlantic Bar however had panache, bathed in a sea of red light with its own band playing with gusto. The girls there had style, the dancers twirled and stepped to the Latin music. The seamen and other visiting firemen would pick their favourites and court them with drinks and compliments. It was a scene that Toulouse Lautrec would have favoured. The girls were mostly pretty, smartly dressed, fluent in English, enjoying repartee, and they had their favouites too. Often the music and dancing would go on to four in the morning. One of my abiding memories is of Spanish marines from a warship, dressed in white canvas uniforms with leather belts and shoulder straps, samba dancing with the Lisbon girls whose white flouncy petticoats swirled to the music. 'Me vota baillar El Bayonne' the singer cried as the tempo increased and the Spaniards' drill boots crashed on the floor. The marines clapped and stamped their boots faster and faster causing God knows what damage to the floor while the English and Danish merchant seamen applauded and sent up drinks for all concerned when they had finished. As we found ourselves in Lisbon every three weeks, I got to know the city well enough to be content to sit on the deck admiring the graceful sailing cargo boats with their barefoot crews, that sailed up and down the broad Tagus. A lot of cargo was ferried up and down the Portuguese coast by this method and often we ourselves would load cargo over the side to them for shipment to smaller ports. There was always bustle on the quayside, a market to shop for fruit and souvenirs and a plentitude of bars to quench one's thirst. I got to know the proprietor of a small bar opposite the station where the third engineer and myself would commence our carousels.

Eventually we got into the habit of going across the road at lunchtime with the proprietor calling me 'Telegraphista socialista' and the third engineer 'Engineiro conservidor'. We discussed politics avidly and I realized that the proprietor was a socialist refugee from the harsher regime of General Franco. I arranged to bring him socialist literature in Spanish from Colletts' bookshop in London. There was the difficulty that both he and I would be in severe trouble if caught, and indeed we would have faced prison sentences. The next trip I came supplied with copious quantities of literature. Our friend the bar owner came aboard for a drink. There are always quantities of Playboy type magazines, 'wanker's' manuals really, so we inserted the socialist literature between several of these and went ashore. The policeman on the gangplank looked at the girlie magazines, rolled his eyes salaciously and waved us on, glad to have seen something to relieve his boredom. Salazar's policeman on the ship was no prude but a patrolling matellot on the beach at Estoril was. I used to take a sixpenny train ride in the afternoons for a swim at the fashionable resort at Estoril and one day while sunbathing, clad only in trunks, the armed patrolling sailor beckoned me to cover my chest. At first I didn't realize what he was saying, but he pointed at my shirt and didn't leave until I had put it on. Across the road at the Casino the expensive prostitutes operated without hindrance but the sight of an uncovered male chest was an affront to Catholic decency. Many years later I was lucky enough to attend a conference of the Socialist International, hosted in the Algarve by the Socialist party of Portugal. I was able to relate my literature smuggling story to my hosts and felt I had contributed my tuppenceworth to the success of the Portuguese revolution. I visited the dockside bar now proudly renamed 'Bar April 25th' in honour of the day of the revolution. Manuel, now over seventy, did not recognise me after a lifetime of seafaring customers but now he can buy his socialist paper on the corner, instead of risking arrest smuggling it ashore.

The day in 1954 that India marched into the Portuguese colony of Goa we docked in Lisbon. One could feel the tension in the air compounded by the hysterical broadcasts from Radio Liboa. Portugal had no way of defending the tiny enclave which had been declared a part of metropolitan Portugal. Probably there was a case for a referendum for the citizens of Goa to decide their own destiny, but, as the citizens of fascist metropolitan Portugal were not allowed the vote, it would have been incongruous to give it to the Goanese. Anyway the Portuguese took the seizure of Goa as a national affront, compounded by the fact that there was nothing they could do about it.

That evening I went ashore to witness a huge demonstration of national anger in Lisbon's Black Horse Square. People were rushing about, faces suffused with anger, weeping openly and shouting 'Viva Portugal' at the top of their voices. A dark skinned man in a turban would have been surely lynched in Lisbon that night. Elderly men with white waxed moustaches, dressed in nineteenth century uniforms hung with medals and swords, were carried shoulder high by packs of screaming men and women. It was an outburst of blind nationalist hysteria that I was to witness in Ulster some sixteen years later in the guise of civil rights demonstrations, but that's another story. Twenty years later in the May 25th revolution, Portugal walked away from its colonies without so much as a cheep of protest from her citizens, but I suppose this time the demagogues were kept away from the radio.

Three enjoyable months on the Portuguese coast came to an end when my six months' training period was completed. Looking back on that time I remember often the enjoyable hedonistic times in Lisbon, a city such as London would have been in Dicken's time, even though I know, for the Portuguese working class, life must have been a fearful nightmare of repression and drudgery. I salved my conscience for my hedonism by helping the young Communists in Hampstead to sell their paper round the doors while we were berthed in Shadwell Basin, even though I disagreed with them on many issues, such as lack of freedom of expression in the U.S.S.R. Spain and Portugal are now favourite holiday destinations, both democracies with ruling socialist parties returned from exile, and life is a hundred times better for their citizens, but in the fifties they were colourful, isolated, unexplored and even the dead hand of fascism and the Church could not stifle the vibrancy of the people.

I go to Portugal often and find that much of Lisbon's beautiful buidings and squares are unchanged. I sit in a cafe in Black Horse Square and remember my youth and the Spanish marines dancing in the Atlantic Bar.

THE CURSE OF THE MICAPE

Now it was time to report to Marconi in East Ham for reassignment. By this time I had heard of the hazard of being sent to the Indian coast for two years, where alcohol was illegal and where you were stranded with no way of getting home. As luck would have it the depot clerk told me to be prepared to fly to Bombay. When I refused the assignment I was promptly dismissed for breaking the union agreement. However I registered with the union as a freelance operator and a boring month of unemployment followed. I found that the 'home is the sailor' syndrome soon wears thin when the money runs out. Eventually a telegram arrived from a Greek shipping company offering a job on the S.S.Micape which was docked at Liverpool. Without the price of a taxi I lugged my suitcases up to the agent's office in Liverpool. There I met the master of the Micape with a freckle-faced youth who was signing on as an A.B. The captain, whose name was Willard, signed me on at a rate of £26 a month when the freelance rate was £40, but being unfamiliar with freelance work I didn't know this, and indeed I later realised that it was possible to negotiate one's own rate taking account of the fact that the ship could sail without a Captain but could not sail without a Radio Officer. 'The ship's a floating slum, Sparks, she's really under the arm' said freckle face in his Liverpool patois. Captain Willard I will remember as a hound of misfortune for the rest of my days, but that's another story.

The Micape was everything the A.B. said it was, a mass production ship built in Canada during the war for the Atlantic convoys. These ships and American Liberty ships could be bought at the end of World War II for £100,000 and clear their outlay in a year's trading. The fortunes of Messiers Goulandris, Kulakundis, Embericos and a few other millionaires were based on these government ships. The quarters were comfortable enough but the decks were soaked with fish oil to stop rust which tramped into all the carpets. The radio room was an annex of the chart room which was convenient for conversations with the mates but the radio equipment turned out to be woefully inadequate. The main receiver and transmitter had been made in Canada under licence from Marconi and the transmitting frequencies allocated to the ship wandered all over the dial and it was very difficult to raise a coast station on short wave. I was to discover this after leaving the range of the medium wave which was about 100 miles from shore in day time. The articles we signed said LEFO, which is an acronym for Lands End radio for orders, which meant the owners would telegraph the ship via Lands End radio when we passed it. The captain had told us that we were bound for Canada to load general cargo for the U.K. but a more experienced seaman than myself would have known that the route for Canada lay around the north coast of Ireland. However when we came in range of Lands End radio the telegram I copied read 'Proceed Buenos Aires roads for loading port. Load 17,000 long tons grain for Gdansk'. I was engulfed with dismay as I realised that the ship would not be back to the U.K. or between the rivers Brest and Elbe, where the Merchant shipping act said it was legal to pay off. It was even possible to be away for two years before the ship owner would be required to change the crew.

The ship's saloon found me eating with a brown third engineer who originally was from Indonesia and carried a Dutch passport, and the second engineer whose engineer's gold bars were green with verdigris and whose head appeared to be caked in dirt. The chief engineer was a Canadian Scot who had worked most of his life on the Great Lakes and could find nothing good to say about Britain. Captain Willard's pockmarked face and pale watery eyes betrayed an insecurity associated with his lack of command experience. The Chief Officer was a middle aged lowland Scottish batchelor of a type often found at sea. Having gone to sea at an early age he had lost contact with the friends of his youth and with the death of his parents the ship became his only home. He had become a sea gypsy. A decent lonely man whose bible was the Reader's Digest and who loved to argue the toss on subjects about which neither the Reader's Digest nor himself knew much. The second mate was the most experienced seaman of the lot having been in the Royal Navy in the lower deck and passing his second mates ticket by self study. He was a Gaelic speaking Harris Islander and every penny was a hostage for the fishing boat and house he needed at home. The crew were mostly Bootle boot boys, all with D.R's (declined to report) on their seamen's books.

Sailing on to the West African port of Dakar was uneventful enough, except to say that our Captain exhibited a tendency to extreme mateyness once past the Canaries. He would invite members of the crew, with whom he had business, for a drink in his cabin. When the business in hand was completed he would slide closer on the settee and then drop the claw. When my turn came I saw the move coming and extricated myself by saying I was due on watch, knowing that his nervousness about running the ship would overcome his homosexual tendencies. One night on the 8 to 10 watch I smelt a sickly musk perfume in the radio room but as my back was to the door I didn't see the Captain come in and was unaware of his presence until I felt a hand reach down the back of my shorts. I spun round and delivered a smart clip to the Captain's jaw and watched him stagger out through the door, full drunk. The freckle-faced A.B. I had met in the agent's office was on the wheel and when I looked into the wheelhouse the Captain had wrapped himself round him like a rug and was 'humping away'. The terrified and shocked youth was steering the ship with the captain on his back and unable to budge. 'Third mate! Third mate!' shouted freckle face, but the third mate had decided that there was something requiring his attention far out at sea and pretended not to notice. I pulled the drunken skipper off the sailor's back and steered him back to his cabin, muttering about reports to the owners. This was enough to sober him up and we had no more bother from him that night. Indeed it was a difficult situation, being placed under the command of a man who was not far short of being a homosexual rapist.

  Three long weeks accross the South Atlantic towards Argentina, with other shipping thin on the ground, I tried to raise Buenos Aires radio on 4, 8, and 12 kcs, all to no avail. I called and listened out repeatedly all through one watch and into another and all through the night. I made a general call to all ships in the area to relay my message but heard no reply. I knew that the whole ship depended on me receiving the loading orders and blisters appeared on my morse key fingers as the tension in the chart room increased. Eventually we approsched Ricolada, the island pilot station in the Estuary in the River Plate. I called B.A. radio on 500 kcs (medium wave) and the long awaited reply QRU (I have a message for you). The pilot boat was already at sea heading towards us as I copied the telegram 'Proceed Bahia Blanca, load 17,000 longtons for Gdansk'. As I rushed into the chart room with the still scribbled telegram, the pilot boat pulled alongside expecting a rope ladder to take the pilot on board. Unfortunately the port of Bahia Blanca was two hundred miles further down the coast and not in the River Plate estuary at all. The first mate quickly laid off a new course while the skipper looked out the port window for all the world like he was not expecting a pilot boat and hadn't seen it.

The course set, he telegraphed the engine room 'full steam ahead'. To my dying day I will never forget the look of surprise followed by fury on the fat Argentine pilot's face as our ship steered past him at full speed. He probably had been called from his siesta to take this assignment and showed his displeasure by jumping up and down gesticulating with forearm in the Latin symbol for 'fuck you', and with his forefingers on his forehead in the world wide symbol for cuckold. All this was a source of delight and amusement to our Liverpool sailors with the deck officers' embarrassed and blank faced. Later I received a reprimand from the World Telecommunications Union for excess calling, but the Italian ship that reported me did not offer to relay my message.

Today I understand that all important communications are relayed by satellite, effectively deskilling the radio officer and, as I write, the radio officer's function at sea will be finished in three years, ending the tradition of progress, often dramatic, and the frequently heroic story of the merchant marine communications.

ARGENTINA

Argentina in the fifties was perhaps like France in the thirties. Old prewar Fords and Buicks, broad brimmed fedoras against a backdrop of art deco architecture, incongruous milk bars and ancient tramcars made Bahia Blanco 'worth seeing but not worth going to see', as Dr. Johnston said. Puerto Engineiro White, called after the Scottish engineer who built it, provided our berth some ten miles from the city. A collection of grain silos, and railway sidings, surrounded by two streets of wooden houses containing a couple of restaurants, provided our immediate not very inspiring environment. A hot scorching wind blew across the pampas which for the most part appeared to be uncultivated. The land was as flat as a billiard table as far as the eye could see, consisting of mile after mile of tufted scutch grass. The day we docked our Captain was rushed to hospital with an appendicitis, giving rise to the theory that he was a Jonah, meaning that disaster attended everything he touched. The other theory expounded was that he was really very lucky in that if we had been at sea a day longer he would have died of peritonitis. Be that as it may, it now devolved on the shoulders of the chief mate to run the ship and load the cargo.

Our amiable chief mate hated the responsibility and now having access to the ship's liquor bond he proceeded to drink it dry to sooth his frayed nerves. He was often joined in his drinking bouts by our grizzled Dublin bosun who in turn neglected the supervision of the sailors. The sailors and firemen, having drunk all the money that they could draw, sold their cold weather clothes to the Argentine dockers who much admired the English cloth. The dry hot pampas wind generated a monumental thirst that our crew, most of whom had been sacked from other ships, slaked with abandon. They would slip off in ones and twos, often after breakfast and return drunk at lunchtime. One day I was in my bunk in the afternoon, sheltering from the heat and enjoying a siesta, when I was rudely disturbed by the chief steward and a drunken and disgruntled fireman rolling over and over on the deck, into my cabin; their hands were round each others throats and each one was trying to throttle the other. Apparently the fireman had returned from the cantina to find that his lunch was cold and showed his displeasure by throwing it in the steward's face. The chief steward, who was at least twenty stone, fell on top of him and the fireman, to avoid being crushed, rolled over and over out of the steward's room into the alleyway and into my cabin. Another time when the ship ran out of pesos, an angry crowd of sailors and firemen advanced on the midship's accommodation with the avowed intention of lynching the officers. The chief mate mollified them by promising to get more money from the agents and eventually they retreated, still muttering threats. This was my first experience of mob rule, the effect of which seems to deprive normally sensible men of their ability to think and act rationally. I saw it frequently in later life in Belfast during the civil rights riots, when drunken men would stagger out of pubs to stone buses, starting a sequence of events that would leave hundreds of people dead, injured and homeless.

The crew were mostly Liverpool Irish, fiercely anti-communist, but resentful of anyone who appeared to be more privileged than themselves. Marx would have classified them as lumpen proleteriat but, for all that, in sobriety some of them could be very interesting and entertaining as they related anecdotes, usually connected with drunken scrapes in various parts of the world.

One of the firemen, a middled aged quiet little man, who made no concessions to climate or custom, wearing as he did a duncher dexter and muffler, made his way to Bahia to buy presents for his family. An incongruous and obviously British figure gazing in the shop windows, the Argentine police arrested him for creating a disturbance. No disturbance of course had occurred, but the agents were informed that a bribe in the region of fifty pounds would be necessary for the fireman to avoid prison. We had a whip round to raise the sum to have him freed and it was thus that Peron's police supplemented their pay. On another occasion McLean, the second mate, directed a visiting engineer from another ship to my cabin on the grounds that we were both from the island of Ireland. These were the days before the conflict between the two nations in Ireland had re-erupted. The engineer was from Cork, incoherently drunk and carrying a flagon of wine, although it was only early afternoon. As I know little about Cork and the engineer's accent was impenetrable, I found the conversation hard going. He was from the London Greek ship ahead of us and apparently they had been away from the U.K. for nearly two years. Drunkeness is a common result of prolonged isolation and this poor man was an obvious casualty of the exploitation of merchant seamen at that time, which forced them to be away from home for up to two years at a time. Anyway, I decided that the best way to terminate this difficult conversation was to have urgent business ashore. The engineer followed me ashore and I watched his faltering steps back to his own ship.

The next day I had a visit from a posse of Harbour policemen headed by a moustachioed captain who spoke enough English to ask me to accompany him to the station. Knowing the form of the Argentine police I was terrified and our returned Captain did not help matters by shouting from the bridge, 'Tell them the truth Sparkie'.

The captain led me into the police office where the blanket covered corpse of the Irish engineer lay in a foetal position in the corner. Apparently he had been fished out of the dock between his ship and the pier and the Indian sailor on the gangway watch denied seeing or hearing anything, probably as he was asleep. I explained that I had met the man only once when he visited my cabin uninvited and that I had last seen him staggering towards his own ship. It turned out that our third mate, who was not over endowed with common sense, had been on board the other ship when the police arrived to investigate the death and had volunteered the information that the Micape Sparks had been talking to him in his cabin. 'Sparks also comes from Ireland'.

The police captain was puzzled by the fact that we were both listed as British citizens and I did not want to complicate the matter by saying that the engineer was not in fact a British citizen but was an economic migrant from Eire working on a British ship. Eventually the captain wrote down British citizen of Irish descent which seemed to satisfy him. I breathed a sigh of relief that the policeman had not heard of the national conflict in Ireland otherwise a ready motive would have been handed to an obviously ambitious minor official in a backwater awaiting his big break. My mind was racing, would release money be demanded from the agents? Would my shipmates pay the bribe? It was not until I was safely back on board that I could spare a thought for the poor Cork man drowned so far from home. The man had been in a helpless condition and had probably slipped on the gangplank, unseen by the Lascar on duty, probably because he was asleep.

In Argentina at that time Eva Peron, the former courtesan and wife of the dictator, had illegalized prostitution, which, when you think of it, was like the Pope abolishing Christmas. The Argentine port police however, always eager to make a dishonest peso, acted as procurers for the seamen. Our crew were more interested in drink than the opposite sex, so they did very little business with us, which perhaps was the reason the fireman was arrested and I was taken for questioning.

There was a club run by the Missions to Seamen in Puerto Engineiro White which had nightly dances to records played on an old fashioned gramaphone. These non-atmospheric affairs were attended by the well bred daughters of British families in Bahia who plied us with mugs of tea and, where there was a hearty welcome, a seat and a hymn book. These Flying Angel soirees reminded me of the Dramatic Society socials at Orangefield church and were about as exciting as watching paint dry. I met a very tall and likable English girl there whose daddy was 'with' the railway company which had been British owned at one time. There is a sizable British community in Argentina and this man decided he was better off in Argentina, which was indeed true for middle class people at that time. He was insistant about one thing though, he wanted his daughters to marry men of British origin. This however was not where I saw my future so the relationship did not prosper. The British expatriates had their club in Buenos Aires, as indeed had the Irish, who fielded hurley and gaelic football teams. There are also Spanish speaking descendants of Irish immigrants in the camp or 'campo,' meaning field or pampas. I later met a Welsh speaking Argentine in Venezuela who spoke no English. He was my cousin's headmaster in the oil company school in Maracaibo and both she and I had to speak to him through a Spanish speaking interpreter.

On New Year's Eve I went ashore and, going through the dock gate, I heard the sound of the long Ulster vowel. It was an A.B from the Muswell Hill, the London-Greek ship moored ahead of us. He came from Islandmagee, where every house flies a merchant navy flag on the 12th of July. We decided to see the New Year in and drink to our homeland in a cowboy bar with horses tethered to the rail. Later a meal was ordered with bottles of Argentine champagne. More champagne was ordered and the 'Sash' was sung as only an Islandmagee can sing it. Cognacs were ordered and depatched with copious draughts of beer until after the last hour of the old year. The arrival of the New Year coincided with the emptying of our wallets.

The Muswell Hill was nearby, but my ship had moved to a berth five miles up the river. My compatriot offered me a berth on board his ship but I had a much better idea. There was an empty carriage in the railway marshalling yard. I bedded down on a comfortable bench seat and bade my friend goodnight and a Happy New Year. I was next to see him in Gdansk at the other side of the world.

I slept soundly enough and wakened to a gentle rhythm and rocking. The rhythm was the sound of iron wheels on railway tracks and the rocking was the ticket collector wakening me up. I looked round to see telegraph poles and houses flashing by and puzzled and disgusted swarthy faces all around me. 'Buenos Aires express Senor Billete por favor.' Of course I had no ticket, no money, and my head ached and my tongue refused to budge from the roof of my mouth to which it cleaved. I threw myself on the mercy of the ticket collector, showed him my upturned palms in mute helplessness, and hoped for the best. I reckoned that Buenos Aires was three hundred miles away so I was in for a six hour journey with an Argentine jail staring me in the face when I arrived. To my surprise the ticket collector smiled and said 'Uno momento Senor' and departed in the direction of the engine driver. He returned ten minutes later as the train stopped at a small station. With all the eyes of the passengers on me, the ticket collector guided me to the bare platform where the stationmaster was opening the ticket booth. 'Uno billette para el puerto', said the ticket collector. The ticket collector purchased a ticket for me and then led me across a village square where a small cafe was just opening. 'Uno cafe solo y dos aspirinas para mi amigo.' He paid for the black coffee and aspirins and shook my hand. 'Feliz nuevo anno Senor.' I managed to get my tongue round the response as he walked back to his train. I will never forget the kindness of that man who was intelligent enough to size up the situation and good hearted enough to take remedial action. I have since regretted not being quick witted enough to get his name so I could repay his kindness in some way.

I arrived back at the port, found my ship and then took to my bunk. For the rest of our stay in Argentina I spent my days at a small beach nearby, watching the working class families from Bahia take their leisure, always on the outside looking in. Nearby was a modest beach club which, although fenced off, offered a view of barbecues of whole sheep with middle class people singing and dancing to the music of guitars. I thought it would be lovely to join them, but then I thought of the havoc that would be wrought by the likes of our crew in such a place. Such is the loneliness of the seafaring life. Soon, however, we were loaded and on our way.

SOUTH ATLANTIC BLUES

The Micape catalogue of misfortune started soon after we left Argentine waters headed for West Africa. Our Captain recovered from his operation in Bahia, promptly fell down the companionway and lamed himself. We didn't know it at the time but he had cracked his heel bone, the one beneficial aspect of it being that it also cramped his homosexual importuning. Some days out, I saw the mates and engineers peering at a crack in the metal deck which opened and shut as the ship lurched in the South Atlantic rollers. To me it appeared serious as the ship could be riven in two, given severe storm conditions. The Captain had no idea of what to do, but one thing he would not do was to inform the owners. To do so would be to admit his own incompetence. Eventually the second mate came up with the remedy. This entailed building a strong concrete box over the crack to stop it from spreading. This indeed was done and as concrete bonds with steel it held firm for the rest of the trip. The second mate had probably washed more salt water out of his socks than most of us, and being brought up on the Isle of Lewis with the roar of the Atlantic in his ears, this knowledge would have been gleaned from generations of fishermen and seamen.

Our next shock came just a few hours steaming from Dakar in French West Africa. A whey faced third engineer rushed on deck, putting as much distance as he could between himself and the engine room. A vital component of the engine, called something like a piston shoe, had overheated. In fact it had become red hot, threatening to explode the engine and us with it. The chief engineer ordered a fireman to shut down the engine and our ship wallowed in the Atlantic roll like a sick cow. A telegram to the agents in Dakar fetched out a tug to tow us in to the harbour, costing the Greeks several thousand pounds in salvage costs. Again I felt myself a useful member of the crew being in a position to summon help when the need arose. French engineers and Senegalese workmen swarmed aboard in Dakar and, with blocks and tackle, curses and negroid grunts hauled the huge overheated piston shoe on deck. This meant a two week wait in this colourful and interesting African port.

The harbour wall encircled about five square miles of water with finger-like piers accommodating ships of all shapes and sizes. Africans in colourful robes were always coming and going, bad mouthing the French and declaring their undying affection for the English. Indeed the French technicians and officials affected an imperious attitude towards them, an attitude that suggested that the Africans didn't exist. I knew that Senegal supplied much of France's colonial army, but the cultural background and history of the place were unknown to me. The shops sold postcards of an African woman cleaning her baby by licking its bottom, and I have threaded my way through women squatting in the street to defecate, but perhaps this is a reflection of French urban sanitation rather than African backwardness. When we drew our 'subs' we found that the five franc note bore a picture of a bare breasted African girl which prompted the fourth engineer to ask for a hundred franc note on the grounds that it would surely depict a couple copulating. Dakar harbour, with the sounds of crickets and odd howls of creatures of the nearby jungle, the bright sunlight and the bustle of the port traffic, was indeed a pleasant place to sit on deck with a book and a beer. One of our firemen was an elderly alcoholic who had served in the Canadian Army in the first world war. He was a harmless creature whose mind was addled but, as the chief engineer said, was 'Verra handy wi the fires'. He had an unfortunate fantasy of believing he was back in the army, mounting guard with a broom stick and pacing up and down the firemen's alley way. However, when we were at sea he got on with his job and bothered no one. An African set up a beer stall, much to his delight, as it saved him a walk ashore and soon the fireman was in a drunken fantasy. He emerged from the engine room where he was meant to be helping the shore gang, gave a leap on to the hatch cover where he executed his own version of a Scottish reel. He was originally from Scotland so the reel was accompanied by hoots and shouts. The Africans on the quay gathered in dozens, falling about laughing, even tripping over their long robes in merriment. The fireman, oblivious of their existence, felt it was time to go ashore to slake his thirst again. At his first step on to the gangway the crowd of now terrified Africans took to their heels, lifting their robes the better to run. It was an amazing sight to see twenty or so terrified blackmen fleeing the presence of our poor addled fireman. Later I was told that Africans believed mad men are possessed of the devil and can inflict grievous harm by their touch. Anyway our fireman composed himself sufficiently to pass the now empty beerstall whose owner had fled with the rest, to the first cafe outside the dock gates.

I passed him there sitting under a parasol on the pavement and when he spotted me he sprang to his feet and gave a salute worthy of a guardsman. I was embarrassed but God only knows what the startled French people round about him thought.

Dakar was like Paris in the tropics, with smart pavement cafes frequented by French expatriots and safari suited African middle class. Like Paris it was horribly expensive until we discovered that the drinks cost half the price in African restaurants. The noise, the colour, and the animation of the African cafes were more atmospheric if one didn't mind the odd begger displaying his stumps, or the pedlars with armfuls of leather goods made in Lyons or Marseilles. It was possible to talk freely in English without being understood, but on one occasion the third mate and myself were approached by an African youth who rejoiced in the name of Moses. Moses was from Gambia and spoke English in a slow African way which evoked sympathy or even pity. He carried a huge pile of testimonials from ships' captains of all nationalities. Moses was, they all stated, a reliable, conscienious and intelligent ship's watchman who had performed his duties diligently in ports up and down the West African coast. Would we recommend him to our Captain? Knowing our Captain's proclivities we wouldn't do that to our worst enemy, but we agreed to recommend him to our chief mate who was in charge of ship's security. He was duly hired as ship's watchman, took up residence in the sickbay, and positioned himself on the gangway every night. The first sign that all was not well was when one of the sailors placed his foot in a homeric African stool curled in the basin of the sailors shower. Joe Brophy, the kindly Dublin Bosun, saved Mose's skin from the wrath of the offended sailor and then advised Moses to go ashore to the toilet as there was no shower there to be confused with the toilet. Part of the watchman's duty was to waken the Bosun at six a.m., who in turn would rouse the deck crew to wash the decks before breakfast. The deck crew's morning task completed, it was the function of the Bosun to waken the chief mate to report that all was ship-shape and 'Bristol fashion'. The chief mate's cabin was two along from my own, and this morning I heard a ferocious Dublin oath followed by the unmistakable sound of knuckles meeting skin and bone. The unfortunate Moses couldn't tell the time and had hazarded a guess that was two hours out and called the Bosun at four a.m!

The Bosun had only looked at his watch after rousing the crew and calling the mate. Poor Moses' retribution from the Bosun was immediate and physical. I heard Moses was sacked after that but still hung around the ship where the cook would give him cups of tea and the odd Liverpool 'sarny'. Moses was doing his best to survive and I felt sorry for him and yielded to his request for a further reference to add to his already copious collection. I signed it as Radio Officer which would not impress any potential employer, but it seemed to make him happy and mollify him for the hurt of being fired. It was not his fault that a shower looked like a French toilet with the hole in the middle, or that a four looked much the same as a six. Moses took us to an African dance hall one night and that was an experience I shall never forget. The taxi carrying Moses, myself and two shipmates turned off the smart boulevards of Dakar into an endless maze of corrugated iron and packing case huts, built at random in what appeared to be desert.

After some miles we arrived at a corrugated iron hall, much like a Hibernian hall in the Sperrin mountains. No white face was to be seen inside, but a sea of robed, black bodies swayed and stamped to the music of a string band. We were shown to our table by a dignified and courteous waiter who seemed to double as M.C. and band leader. We ordered beer in French while Moses whispered something in his tribal language which I hoped was an explanation that we were British seamen and not French soldiers. The beer was drinkable and cheap and soon our feet were tapping to the African music which was quite intricate, with a heavy beat. Being unable to hear music with a beat without experiencing a strong desire to dance, I plucked up my courage to ask a bare foot Negress to take the floor. This she did and I am sure we made an incongrous pair as I tried to give her the lead as taught in Betty Staff's School of Ballroom Dancing. I looked around and there was the third mate whose confidence outstripped his competence, dancing all over the bare feet of his unfortunate partner with his size eleven beetle crushers. His partner had a stoic expression on her face as if it was the lot of a subjected colonial race to suffer such pain and indignity in silence. However, we had drawn attention to ourselves which moved the patron to move the tilly lamp from our table to the other side of the dance hall. Soon a drunken African came to our table, who claimed to be the chef to the British ambassador and the holder of the Victoria Cross won with the King's African Rifles in Burma. As he did speak English there must have been at least some substance to his story so we bought him a drink. Numerous English speaking Africans joined our table and we listened to the most unlikely stories in a convivial manner. Some claimed to have travelled to the United States where they recognised distant cousins by their tribal scars. I saw a Senegalese film many years later which told of a French Colonial Unit, returning to Senegal in cast off U.S. uniforms at the end of World War II, to be confused with American black soldiers stationed there. I gather that a strong interest developed in Senegal then in the position of Blacks in America and their origin in West Africa.

The memory that abides with me is of people who exaggerated their success to the point of fantasy, compensating for a sense of inferiority induced by living in a colonial society. Independance, whatever ills in the form of corruption and military dictatorship it brings, must surely restore a sense of self eseem that white patronage destroyed.

Dakar's busy harbour was an unending source of interest in the diverse range of shipping traffic it contained. The jabber of dockers, traders and even the beggars who thronged the quays was a source of interest and amusement. One day a huge French troopship, filled with Senegalese troops, docked. It was returning them from duty in France and some of them cradled coffee coloured infants in their arms, but with no sign of their mothers. I was reminded of this scene when I saw the film 'Papillon', about the French gangster who escaped from Devil's Island. In the film the route from the prison to the prison ship was lined with black soldiers with fixed bayonets. I wonder if this reliance on mercenary colonial soldiers was a reflection of the government's fear of the army siding with the prisoners and letting them escape.

Another troopship arrived with little brown men incongruously dressed in khaki turbans, topical shirts and shorts and blue American baseball boots. These soldiers were Moroccan Ghoums, fearful little men who were returning from Vietnam, where they were paid 5 francs for every enemy ear they presented to their officers. The French radio technician who was trying unsuccessfully to trace the fault in our transmitter told me how the people of France were delighted that the war in Vietnam was over and the killing stopped. Little did either of us guess that Uncle Sam was to take over with its military advisors, and slaughter hundreds of thousands in an effort to turn the clock back.

POLISH SEAPORT OF GDYNIA, NEAR GDANSK

FAREWELL DAKAR - HELLO GDANSK

The engine repaired, we left Dakar en route to Gdansk via the Kiel canal in Germany. The snow was thick on the ground when we docked in Brunsbuttle at the entrance to the canal, and our acquired African cat associating the cold with the ship, scooted ashore at the first opportunity. I often wondered how she survived the German winter. Our Captain, whose first command was dogged by so many misfortunes, warmly greeted a Scotsman who came aboard, thinking that he must be the ship's agent in Kiel. To his chagrin the Scot turned out to be a replacement master come to relieve him of his command. Captain Willard had all of half an hour to pack his gear, finalize his accounts and leave for Hamburg airport. A casual labourer would have been given more notice and consideration. The shipowners rely on officers to achieve the necessary qualifications to maintain and sail their ships and then hire and fire them at literally a moment's notice. At the time of writing, the collective arrangements for study leave and federation waiting pay have all but been abolished, most Merchant ships are now 'flagged out' with flags of convenience and only the supervising authority being the insurers. At my time at sea there were around seven thousand vessels flying the red ensign but now there are only five hundred. The new Captain was rumoured by the crew to have had two ships sunk under him, and the consensus was that the Micape was costing too much to maintain and that the owners would be better off to be rid of her. As it was, we sailed through the Kiel Canal without the new Captain appearing on the bridge or appearing in the saloon. The steward said every time he brought his food to the cabin the Captain appeared to be drunk.

Later it transpired that the entire ship's bond, meant to last an entire voyage, had been drunk by him alone in three weeks. We took on a Polish pilot in Swinoujie to navigate us through a minefield to the port of Gdansk. The Captain never put in an appearance. The river Vistula flows quickly, murkily and deeply through the village of Novyport where a dozen freighters were lined up at grain silos. Polish army officers in green uniforms cursorily inspected our rooms and checked us off against the crew list. They were pleasant young men, university graduates, doing their military service at the time.

An armed guard was stationed on the crane, on the tugboat and on the gangway. Clearly the war with the nationalist armed bands was not over. Some years later the great film maker Waijda was to make the poignant film 'Ashes and Diamonds' about this post-war period of Polish history.

The Poles were cheerful and friendly, speaking German which seemed to be the lingua franca in these parts. Puff Leyland's classes at Belfast 'Inst' came to my rescue and I was able to discern that we were five miles from Gdansk. Darkness, snow and yellow street lamps combined, with rubble remaindered from World War II, to give an atmosphere I had never experienced before. A feeling of intense Slavic soulfulness engulfed me as a military lorry full of young soldiers passed slowly, the young soldiers singing a melancholy folk song. Eventually a tramcar appeared like a yellow beacon through the dark and snow. It was packed with dockers on their way home to Gdansk from the port. One of them spoke to us in English with a pronounced Scottish accent. He told us he had been in General Anders' Polish Army, was stationed in Stirling for a year, and had come home to Poland after the war in spite of blandishments to stay in Britain. All the dockers wore the same grey quilted garments which were apparently issued free to outdoor workers. They were drab, no doubt, but very serviceable for the continental winter. The tramcar clanked through the rubble lined roads and when we reached the city centre all we saw was one neon sign spelling 'Hotel Orbis'. 'This is the centre of Gdansk, that is the Orbis Hotel and that is the Gdansk railway station', said our ex-soldier friend. Thirty years on we were to see the same railway station and the same hotel flashing across our TV screens as the drama of the shipyard strike and the riots that followed were acted out. The Orbis Hotel was a haven of light in the sea of darkness that was Gdansk. It also was a haven for prostitutes and black marketeers who offered zloties at double the official rate and even offered to buy the clothes off our back. It's a poor heart that never rejoices and at the official rate we managed to sink quite a few beers that were excellent, and even a few cherry brandies. A black beer called porter made me feel at home and with the quick action of the cherry brandy and the friendliness of the people we were soon in good form. We left the Orbis, forsaking the charms of the quite pretty women who quoted their prices in dollars, or rather dollar singular, for that is all they asked. Clambering on board a passing tramcar, we proffered the conductor a fistful of zloties and asked for Novyport. 'Nein Nein! ein andere weg', cried a chorus of concerned Poles.

A young, well dressed man pushed his way forward and addressed us in good English, saying that we were on the wrong tram, but that he would get off with us and show us the way to the port. This he did, taking us through a maze of rubble until we could see the outline of the cranes and ships of the harbour. This was typical of the hospitality and helpfulness from all the Polish people that I was to meet both in Poland and abroad.

Some of the crew arrived back on board minus shirts and ties which they had used to pay for 'short times' with German and Polish prostitutes in a dockside tavern. I went to this place once and found it to be a converted villa, formerly belonging to some German merchant from the prewar time when Gdansk was called Danzig and was a free port inhabited by both Germans and Poles. It was Hitler's claim to Danzig and the Polish corridor which sparked off the second world war. Anyway, the German merchant fled before the advance of the Red Army and it was now a brothel bar. There was a female militia woman resplendant in riding boots and a leather visored cap perched on her luxurious curls, doing traffic duty on the road outside. A swastika was painted on the crumbling remains of the garden wall. Inside there was shabbiness, garish lighting, a bevy of blousy blond prostitutes, leering black firemen and raucous Liverpool sailors from my own ship. I spotted my old friend from Islandmagee and was able to recount my adventure on the Buenos Aires express. Our sailors were drinking beer and vodka as if it was the eve of prohibition, while the sad and garish ladies of the night offered their embraces. The establishment was run by a lanky, lordly looking Pole in riding boots and jodphurs. Some of the women were Poles displaced from the Ukraine while others were Germans washed up on the tide of defeat.

Next morning I heard that our sailors, inflamed by vodka, had started a fight with some German seamen. Apparently the Militia were called and closed the place down. Later I was to see the lordly proprietor trudging through the snow with his packed suitcase. Our Liverpool Catholic crew, who were as chauvinist and anti-Communist as they come, had put an end to the last bastion of private enterprise in Novyport. The public enterprise sector of the Polish economy came into view when a bus arrived to take us into the duty free shop in Gdynia. Gdynia was the purpose built port which gave the newly founded Polish state access to the sea after the first world war. Hitler incorporated it into the Third Reich and renamed it Gotten Hafen.

The Allies gave it back to Poland and divided East Prussia between Russia and Poland so that no future German government would be tempted to join territory with the Polish corridor again. Gydnia appeared not to have suffered so much during the war; its modern port was intact and its art deco buildings dated from the thirties. We crowded through the duty free hard currency shop admiring the Polish-made soft leather shoes, radios, motor bikes, pigskin suitcases and all manner of folk art boxes and embroidery. Here was a veritable Aladdins's cave of goodies, including Scotch whiskey and French brandies which could be obtained by just signing an order form.

The enterprising management realised that seamen's wages are held by the shipowner's head office and, as ship's agents, they could send the invoices to the shipping company who would deduct the item from the seaman's pay. As with the credit card system people tended to spend more than they could afford. Later on the agent came aboard soliciting orders for whiskey, brandy, vodka etc. at duty free prices. Our somnolent Captain awoke to the sound of the deck winch cranking case after case of hard liquor aboard and stirred himself sufficiently to put a halt to it. The disappointed agent had to send back his orders but told the crew he would take orders for hard cash including coinage of any hard currency. This included Argentine pesos and Senegalese francs. Our demented Scots-Canadian fireman was left with a case of minerals which he had ordered as mixers for his ten cases of liquor. Pathetically he went round the ship asking people to search their pockets for loose change in order to make up the price of a bottle of spirits. For myself, I was very dissatisfied with my position on the ship as I had signed on at the Marconi length of service rate instead of the freelance rate which was £14.00 a month more. Ashore at that time £14 was two weeks pay for a tradesman. It seemed everyone else wanted off as well, as the ship seemed to be jinxed, although some of the crew wanted just their wages without having to go to sea for them. Although I was only twenty two years old and in the company of men who had washed more salt water out of their socks than I had sailed over I organised a petition to the owners to be relieved at Kiel on the return journey to Argentina. I got the sailors and firemen to write to the union and wrote to my brother in Belfast requesting a letter to the owners requesting my necessary presence in Belfast. I don't know if any of this worked but one thing that did work was a party of drunken sailors and firemen pulling the Captain out his bed at midnight, demanding to be sent home. The agent told us he had telegraphed the shipping office for a new crew to be sent to Kiel.

The Polish seamens' union sent a bus to the ship one night to take us to the international seamen's club in Gydnia. This was a brightly lit and well appointed building with a library, cinema and nightclub. The dance floor was crowded with sailors of all nationalities and there were pretty girls there in plenty including some Scots lassies who obviously had married Polish soldiers and for whatever reason were carousing at the Interclub. One girl in particular had dark soulful eyes and a crowning glory of auburn tresses piled on her head. I danced with her and found out that she spoke German and was originally from Katowice in Silesia. She had been orphaned during the war and had come to the Baltic coast to find work in the expanding industries the Communist government were setting up and to find accommodation in a former German villa in Sopot. There were other ladies there too, eager for our company and eager for any British cigarettes and pounds that we might have had. In a way it reminded me of the American troops in Ulster during the war, when luxuries were scarce and some of the girls would go with the Americans for the nylons and cigarettes that they gave them.

My friend Lucyna had moved me deeply, and as she escorted me to the bus back to the ship we exchanged addresses. A correspondence lasting two years resulted, but that's another story for another day.

We were to sail for Kiel the next day but loading was incomplete and our departure was postponed. It was not possible to draw any more zloties from the ship as the agent's account had been completed. However, undaunted, I set out for the dock gate where the militia men on duty understood my plight and offered to help. One of them took a biro from my pocket and returned five minutes later with a hundred zloties. Kindly men they were, and when I hear stories of the Communist tyrants in Poland I think of them, knowing that they must have been party members to be in the militia and how unfitting to the stereotype they were. With my hundred zloties I caught the tram, through the ruins, to the now famous railway station in Gdansk where Lech Walensa harangued the crowds. The train took me to Sopot where Lucyna lived. Sopot was a seaside resort which boasted the longest pier in Europe and now was like a western European inner city, with the fine Gothic villas broken into tenements. Lucyna lived in one room in such a house and I noticed that a loudspeaker mounted on a wall, served as a radio. One radio served the whole building, and, presumably, the janitor chose the programmes. We had a pleasant evening at the Interclub, pledged each other undying love in fractured German, and so I sailed on the morning tide, as the songs say.

Most of our crew were confirmed in their anti-Communist views by what they saw in Poland. For myself, I saw evidence of a strong commitment to health provision, in so far as merchant seamen were concerned. Every Polish ship returning to a home port had its entire crew taken to the hospital for a complete health check from head to toe. There were no destitutes and beggars to be seen on the streets as in Spain and Portugal at the time, and everybody seemed well clad and fed. The Polish citizens had a basic right to work, to free health care and free education for their children. The Communist Party carried out a massive programme of industrialisation which gave the Poles full employment for the first time in their history, and if consumer goods were in short supply and luxuries unavailable, that was not the end of the world. This idea has floundered now, with worship at the alter of market forces, but I feel that the wastefulness of unemployment, the stress of men working like Japanese robots in order to buy things that they don't need, while the quality of life in urban environments declines, will eventually force mankind to think again about how the world should be organised.

We left Poland after bunkering at Gdynia and our ship ploughed through the icy Baltic, past the Danish island of Bornholm towards the entrance to the Kiel Canal. We still had no definite word about a relief crew and as I had to have my log signed by the Captain, I made my way to his cabin. This was the first time I had actually seen the Captain at close quarters and I found him to be a pleasant looking man in his fifties. 'I'm in terrible pain from my piles, there's a bottle of whiskey on my desk'. 'Better lay off the spirits then', I said. 'It will only inflame them.' This was to be the last time anyone saw the Captain alive for, half an hour later, he was seen floating in the sea, lying on his back, apparently whistling. Surely a bizarre and untimely death for a man who should have been enjoying a well earned retirement. I had heard the shout 'Man overboard' and rushed to the radio room to start up the transmitter. Our amiable Scots Chief Mate took over command, a job he didn't relish at all. He had a sailor call me to the chart room where I found him with the departed Captain's half bottle of whiskey at his head. 'My doctor warned me about stress', he cried. 'Where the hell are we, anyway?' I needed a position to broadcast a distress signal and eventually the reliable fisherman from Barra calculated our speed and time since leaving Gdynia.

The SOS went out alerting all ships to search for the Captain, but he had disappeared beneath the waves. I read in the English newspapers that his body had fetched up on Bornholm. We then found out that the entire bond of duty free liquor which was supposed to last eight officers for three months, had been consumed by the Captain in three weeks. I have no doubt that the poor man was in agony with the pain of the piles and in a poor mental state due to alcohol abuse. He must have decided on the spur of the moment to make an end of it. I had written a letter to a pal on another ship with whom I had studied, relating the saga of the agitation to get off the ship. I tore this in pieces and flushed them down the toilet. I thought there might be police enquiries about the manner of death of the Captain and I did not want it to be thought that there was foul play. Indeed, the German police boarded in Kiel with the British Consul and both were satisfied with our explanations.

Our relief crew were also waiting at Kiel, all of them drunk and not a bit keen on their new ship. One A.B. had on a long dexter raincoat, belted by a piece of string. He also sported a battered trilby hat which covered a fine featured face, somewhat mottled by drink. He spoke in measured Oxford tones, slurred slightly by drink. Obviously a demoted officer from one of the swanky lines like P&O or Cunard. My mail included a job offer from Union Castle which was unusual as they normally required a first class ticket, while mine was class two. My replacement was a young fellow who had just left Union Castle where he was fourth Radio Officer on a passenger ship. Perhaps he had blotted his copybook, and by a strange co-incidence I was offered his job. A college friend on another London-Greek ship passed the Micape at a distance of fifty yards in Dover Straights, and was unable to raise him. I hate to think of the difficulties the poor fellow had.

The biggest surprise of the day was that Captain Willard had got his old job back. I warned the new radio officer about Willard's proclivities and wished him well. The bus that took us to Hamburg airport at the dead of night was filled with happy faces, only three of the crew electing to remain, which showed that most had a feeling of eventual tragedy which would overtake the ship. I saw the Micape berthed in Newport News, Virginia, a couple of years later and shortly after that she floundered in the

North Sea. All the crew were rescued by Breeches Buoy, all except the hapless Captain Willard. Unlucky to the end, he was hauled aboard with his chest crushed by the tightening rope.

The Merchant Navy ritual of 'paying-off' took place at the shipping office in East London where the Goulandris port captain offered me a job on a Liberian flagged ship leaving Manchester in a fortnight's time. The wages were sixty four pounds a month, which was three times as much as I was earning. Later on I learned I was being used as a Blackleg, as the Greek Radio Officers Union had a minimum rate of eighty four pounds a month.

AROUND THE WORLD

I arrived back in Belfast feeling twenty years older, when in fact I had only been away three short months. It was the trolleybus conductor, who whistled all the time and was on the Castlereagh route for as long as I can remember, who helped me on board with my cases at the bus stop in Albert Square. The dark, Victorian Mountpottinger Road, with its fortress-like police barracks, and the view of the Castlereagh Hills, past the Castle cinema, gave me a comforting feeling of changeless security which had been absent for the previous three months. It being the Easter break, I took a short trip to Achill to stay with Major Freyer, who lived in the beautiful Corrymore house with its view of the Minaun Cliffs and Clare Island.

Staying there at the time was a young student from RADA, Peter O'Toole, who had a tremendous presence. He had a magnificent head which intrigued the locals in Gielty's bar, who would stare at him with unabashed curiosity.

Major Freyer's factotum was a youth from Co. Antrim who was waiting to join the Irish Fusiliers where he hoped to get a commission. He was a pleasant lad with the accents of the Anglo-Irish establishment, but the next I heard of him, he was a Nationalist councillor in Cushendall and eccentric enough to support Sinn Fein. He was shot and wounded by the UVF and apparently lived most of the rest of his life in Japan and had married a Japanese girl.

I was to join a vessel called the Okeanis in Manchester, which was then a thriving port. Sailing to Liverpool in the Ferryboat 'Ulster Princess', I was accosted in the saloon by a gent who spoke in a South London whine. 'The girl over there', he said, pointing to an attractive brunette sitting in the corner, 'is interested in meeting you.' 'She is not interested in me at all, unfortunately', he continued. It occurred to me that this was the action of a pimp, but no pimp he. Mindful of the long, lonely nights at sea ahead of me, I went over to the lady and introduced myself to her. She told me she was a school teacher working in England, and was returning there after a holiday at her family home in Galway in the West of Ireland. At the time I thought it strange that anyone should travel from Galway to England via Belfast, as all the road and rail connections from Galway were via Dublin, which also had a ferry link to Liverpool. Also her conversation was not that of an educated girl, indeed it was hard going to keep her entertained. Eventually nature took its course, swiftly and with little preamble, short and sweet like a donkey's gallop, as you might say.

It was much later that I discovered that MI5 took a great interest in anyone receiving mail from anyone from a socialist country and I had, in the space of two weeks at home, received two letters from Poland. I have no doubt now that this was the reason for this romantic meeting and that the Englishman who arranged the introduction was either MI5 or Special Branch. He obtained what he was looking for, that is the name of my next ship and its whereabouts. I may be wrong, but even then I smelt a rat. It didn't seem like a natural meeting. Since then it has been revealed in Peter Wright's autobiography 'Spy Catcher,' that MI5 are constantly illegally burgling people's homes and tapping their phones if they do not have the same world view as the right wing security services.

I boarded the Okeanis the next day, to probably the biggest culture shock I have had in my life. All the lettering above the doors was in Greek and everybody in sight had swarthy complexions and Zapata moustaches. The chief officer greeted me civilly enough, he had good English, as had the Captain who was married to a Welsh girl and lived in Cardiff. I discovered that several older crew members were also married to Welsh women and that this had to do with Cardiff being the biggest port in the coal trade to pre-war South America. The M.V. Okeanis was a well found post war vessel just bought from a British company, and we were under charter to the Strick Line who carried cargo to the Persian Gulf. The engineers were very busy repairing leaky pipes and had a poor word for the British engineers who had left the engine in a very inefficient condition. The reason for this was probably that they knew that the vessel was sold and spared themselves the trouble of carrying out maintainence. We were loading all sorts of supplies for the oil companies in the Gulf, everything from pipes to cartons of fruit drinks.

I came to understand that the cargo was plundered unmercifully by the crew with the connivance of the officers. There was a blackcurrant drink readily available in every cabin which obviously had been looted from the cargo. The officers ate in a little mess off the chief steward's pantry, while the Captain dined in solitary splendour in the spacious saloon, which was meant for all the officers. There was a refreshing lack of class distinction on board with the mates being addressed by their Christian names, prefixed by the Greek word 'Kapta' meaning, I suppose, Captain, while the engineers were addressed by 'Mastra' which I think was a low grade form of maestro. For myself, I rejoiced in the title 'Marconi', whether as a tribute to the Italian inventor or as a sarcastic comment on the radio officer's ability, I know not. In one of those strange coincidences which link the past with entirely new and strange circumstances, I recognised the Greek engineer superintendent as a former student of Queen's University in Belfast, who used to be very much a man about town. I talked with him about people and places in Belfast and my feeling of isolation was gone.

We sailed down the Manchester Ship Canal, through the detritus of the industrial revolution that scarred the face of England at that time. I explained to the cabin boy, who had never been out of Greece before, that all of England was not so dirty and ugly. Orwell described it well in 'The Road to Wigan Pier', and as I watched the belching chimneys, blackened buildings and filthy streams glide by, I wondered how people could face such squalor day after day. We left the blackened landscape behind us and then the muddy Mersey gave way to the fresh waves of the Irish Sea, and so on to the Straits of Gibralter.

I found out there was one other non-Greek on board and he was a Rangoon born Indian who had the incongrous name of Stamatis. Stamatis spoke good Greek and English after a fashion, and although he lived in Liverpool and was married to an Irish woman, he had worked on Greek ships for thirty years.

All officers in the Greek Merchant Navy are required to pass an exam in English for their certificates, so I found plenty of people willing to converse with me for practise. As I was studying German furiously at the time, I saw no necessity to learn Greek, which of course was a great mistake as another language is easily carried.

The routine of watch keeping, eating and sleeping passed uneventfully until we anchored in Port Said at the entrance to the Suez Canal. Every seaman knows about the bum-boats of Port Said, but the witnessing of what is a water borne 'Souk' is past describing. Dozens of little boats, festooned with carpets, leather goods and trinkets of all sorts, scurry around the anchored ships with their owners shouting the odds in a multitude of languages. Some Arab traders managed to get on board and were scouring the ship looking for scrap metal, ropes and scrap batteries. There happened to be a pile of scrap batteries in the radar house which I agreed to sell for ten shillings. The crafty Arab had me lug the heavy batteries down to the gangway to his boat, whereupon he started his outboard and scurried away without paying me, as fast as his ancient craft would carry him. I had to admire his cheek and no doubt he had played the trick many times before, but he needed the ten shillings more than I did. Some seamen take a delight in flushing the toilets over the bum-boats, knowing that their owners can't come aboard to extract retribution, but this is a cruel trick on poor men trying to scrape a living in harsh circumstances.

The minarets of Port Said shimmering in the desert heat disappeared as we headed up the cuts of sand that make up the Canal. At times we passed villages of biblical aspect with a few date palms and alway khaki clad policemen with .303 rifles patrolling in twos. My brother spent two years in the Canal zone with the Inniskilling Fusiliers when all the towns were off limits and I thought of the monotonous boring experience it must have been. I spotted two Arabs padding through the desert on camels, their white robes flowing in the wind it looked like a Christmas card scene. Indeed in the fifties the Middle East was much as Christ had seen it. Eventually we cleared the Canal and passed through the blistering Red Sea. The Red Sea being narrow we often passed brightly lit passenger ships and fantasized about splendid women in evening dress dancing with the lucky ship's officers. By this time I had got to know the Greeks a bit better and learned that our owner Captain Goulandris had made his fortune from an inter island caique which was sunk in the first world war. On the compensation from this he purchased an American Standard ship which was on the market as 'Navy surplus' and sold for a knock down price. With this as security he managed to borrow enough from the bank to buy other ships and so became a shipping millionaire. Goulandris brothers now rank along with Onassis and Niarchos, owning hundreds of ships and their money and power causes governments to pass special laws and ignore other laws in their favour.

It appeared that most of our sailors came from the Greek islands, especially the big island of Andros, the birthplace of Papa Goulandris. The engineers and firemen tended to be from the cities and there was a mild resentment between them. The Greek engineers considered themselves to be more efficient than their British counterparts, coaxing more knots per ton of fuel out of clapped out engines where the British would simply order new parts. Where there is no tax paid, there are no tax deductions so the owners prefer make do and mend. The non-industrial economy of Greece, where all machinery has to be imported, breeds a special type of engineer who can do this.

The next port of call was Aden, whose jagged rocks surrounded an extinct volcano which immediately reminded me of the pipe band tune 'The Barren Rocks of Aden', often played by the Ulster Rifles Pipe Band. The young English pilot, in spotless whites who took us to Steamer point where we anchored, was quite surprised to be greeted in Ulster- English on a Greek ship but made no effort however to offer me English magazines or newspapers.

UP THE GULF

Some days later we dropped anchor at Muscat which must be one of the most awe inspiring anchorages in the world. Muscat, the capital of the desert kingdom of Oman, is perched on the top of a huge cliff face rising out of the sea at the entrance to the Persian Gulf. The buildings seemed to grow out of the khaki earth and indeed some of them were actually caves. The whole lot was topped off by a Beau Geste like fort at the summit. The huge cliff face was labelled with names of British warships such as H.M.S. Warrior or H.M.S Hercules, signifying in those days who controlled the Gulf. This biblical scene was adorned by ancient Arab dhows, all the same curious shape but in many sizes. The dropping of our anchor was the signal for a fleet of these dhows to head towards us. They were crammed with Arabs in filthy robes and turbans, chequered skirts and bare horny feet. Old men with blind milky eyes turned to the heavens jostled with bearded youths of fourteen to come aboard. This unlikely gang of dockers opened up the hatches and started up the winches to the accompaniment of cries and screams at maximum decibels. They seemed to find it necessary to shout a running commentary of the work progress all the time they were working, even though nobody was listening. The first piece of cargo shifted was a field gun for the Omani army, which they dropped from a height of six feet into the bottom of a very lightly built dhow, which miraculously stayed afloat.

The cargo superintendent, an Englishman, told me that these dockers were rounded up on the street by the Sultan's guard as the ship approached the bay. They worked for two days and nights unloading the cargo and their food was brought after sundown as it was the Moslem fast period of Ramadan. The food consisted of rice and chappaties brought in huge pots which they hunkered down to eat with their hands. Still they managed to shout and scream, with a soldier standing guard with a rifle to make sure they didn't try to swim ashore. I have read since that Marxist guerrillas have tried to topple the Sultan and were suppressed with the aid of the British SAS. I think in the circumstances anyone with a spark of spirit would bcome a Marxist guerilla. We moved on up the gulf to places that have now become states with cities, flags and armies, but then were little more than oilwells with a company store. Ras Tanura, Dohar, Dubai,

Kuwait, had very little else but a pier, a few miles of road and oil wells. As we were carrying stores for the oil companies, unlike the tankers, we were obliged to wait several days at each port. The heat made the metal deck like a furnace wall. A cool drink broke out as sweat on one's chest seconds after taking it. We weren't allowed ashore for fear of fights with the Arabs and couldn't swim for fear of sharks. It was impossible to sleep for long as the bedding became soaked in sweat and the air was stifling. Mail, however, was delivered and I had the consolation of getting an Ulster country paper from the ship's agent in Bahrein who hailed from Warrenpoint in Co. Down. I lay in the stifling heat reading in the Mourne Observer about farmers being fined for having no lights on their bikes in the Mourne country.

Eventually we sailed to Iraq and moored in the Shatt-El-Arab river where the landscape became covered in dark green foliage. These were the date plantations irrigated by the fast flowing, brown and somehow sinister river. At least, although still trapped by the metal furnace of the iron decked ship, there was something to see. Long canoes filled with wailing Arabs would pass, celebrating births, marriages and funerals. At night shots would ring out, some seeming to be quite close. These shots, we were told by the Iraqi pilot, were fired by plantation guards shooting at date thieves. How often they scored a hit I do not know, but one night I saw an Arab shot dead before my eyes. A canoe had drawn up beside the gangway. I went down to investigate and was offered hashish by one of two Arabs in the canoe. I told them to scram and went back up the gangway. There was a British-India ship with an Iraqi army guard on board, moored behind us. A searchlight was beamed on the canoe and an abrupt order in Arabic shouted out, but the canoeist paddled furiously for the shore. A shot was fired and one of the canoeists slipped out of the canoe and floated away with the current of the river. The other made it to the shore. Such was the value of life in the regime of the late King Faisal. Today, as I write, Saddam Hussein has been responsible for the deaths of hundreds of thousands, with his aggression to Kuwait and the futile war he fought to maintain his aggression. The possession of nuclear weapons in the hands of such people is too horrible to contemplate, yet apparently Iraq was well on its way to having some. Eventually I went up the river in the agent's launch to Basra, Iraq's second city and jewel of the Middle East, as the pilot had described it.

Lack of contact with humanity, other than one's colleagues, leaves one nervous, insecure and fragile. In this frame of mind I was pitched into a babble of noise, dust, honking cars and screaming market people competing with beseeching mendicants showing their sores. Startled and confused I hailed a cab and asked to be driven to the best hotel. I pressed a bundle of dinars into the hands of the cabbie and ran, soaking with sweat and disorientated, into the port hotel. The hotel was air conditioned, clean with a touch of eastern luxury and best of all, quiet. I went to my sweet, quiet, air conditioned bedroom and slept for eight hours. I awoke at ten in the evening, shaved and showered, and then, with mounting excitement, ventured out into the warm night air to explore Basra. Attracted by the sound of wailing Arab music I found an open air night club with a succession of girls in diaphanous robes appearing on stage. The girls would wriggle suggestively in the famous Egytian belly dance but one wriggling belly is much like another so I quickly became bored.

Inferior beer at ten shillings a time came close to what an Iraqi worker got for a week's toil in the sun, so although I could afford it, I resented paying it. Rich Arabs in flowing white robes, presumably from the Gulf, sat sipping champagne at seven pounds a bottle, then the equivalent of a British working man's weekly wage. One of the belly dancers sat down beside me, quickly ordered a bottle of champagne, which I just as quickly cancelled. I told her I would buy her a beer which she quickly drank and left. After several beers I became confused again and imagined I was hearing an argument in a Belfast pub between Linfield and Glentoran football supporters. I shook my head and concentrated on the bellydancers. The argument became heated so I turned my chair round to bring in some visual stimulation. The harangues however became louder and I realised that the bronzed young men seated behind me were indeed Linfield and Glentoran supporters. Their faces had the unmistakable stamp of the Scotch-Irish and they turned out to be airmen from the R.A.F. camp at nearby Habaniyah out on their fortnightly pay spree.

One of the airmen, a veteran of the war, was in his thirties and hailed from a district of Belfast known as the Holyland or even sometimes as the exotic sounding Plains of Abraham. This is a respectable working class district whose streets are all named after places in the Middle East, such as Cairo Street or Jerusalem Street. I knew quite a few people there so we discussed the characters of the neighbourhood and found that we had many mutual aquaintances. These airmen, like myself, were away from home a long time without the compensating factor of making another home elsewhere. Such is the nature of service life as well as the Merchant Navy.

Soon, with the flow of beer and the talk of our homeland, we forgot about the bellydancers and the wailing Arab music. We gave a raucous rendition of the 'Sash' much to the annoyance of the Arabs and the management. I gather that the singing of this song was often the precursor of a brawl, as indeed it is in many parts of the English speaking world. However, without damage to either Arabs or property I rejoined my Greek shipmates, well pleased with a refreshing exposure to Ulster dialect and humour.

Since my first hike over the Castlereagh hills at the age of eleven I have always had a burning desire to see what was over the other side. I explored every inch of Ireland before going to sea and took every opportunity to visit new lands and people. However after a short time in Arab lands I found both the land and the people very irritating in spite of my strong philosophy so well put by Rabbie Burns. 'That man to man the whole world o'er a brother is for aw that'. It was impossible to walk very far without feeling weak and parched and indeed there were cola stalls every few hundred yards to replenish your strength, but the incessant clutching of your sleeve by children begging, salesmen selling, and con men conning, the ubiquitous cries of 'Backshish sahib backshish' reduce your disposition to that of a chef in an overheated kitchen with orders for a regiment.

The tales of the foreign legion and the Casbah evaporate with the reality of the Casbah in Basra, which was a walled section of the city containing a brothel. It was out of bounds to the R.A.F. so I reckoned it was unsafe to enter and contented myself with peeking in through the gated entrance. For once I had no desire to explore a new country, but there was an air conditioned port club with a swimming pool which Merchant Navy officers were entitled to use, so, very much against my better nature, I chose the refuge of the colonialist and expatriot, the British Club. Indeed in the half hour walk from the docks to the club it was necessary to make about three stops at the ubiquitous cola stalls to prevent heat exhaustion, all in the cause of drinking an ice cold beer in pleasant surroundings.

Once, in a moment of boredom in the mess on board ship, I idly picked up the second mate's coffee and read a prophecy from the black grounds of the Greek coffee. I had often heard my mother read the tea leaves at home, knew the jargon and some of the signs. I knew that a dog means friendship, that a bell means a wedding, and those I didn't know I made up for myself by dint of converting the shapes in the cup to objects around which I could weave a story. I saw a map of India in the grounds and intimated to old Dimitri that he would be shortly visiting the sub-continent. Later that day the Captain announced that when we had discharged in Basra we would sail for Karachi, which although in Pakistan, is in the Indian sub-continent.

The next morning there was a line of sailors and firemen with used coffee cups at the door of the mess room. I read futures for them which seemed to satisfy them and this harmless form of mendacity continued for the next seven months I was aboard the Okeanos. Indeed I often forgot what I had told them as I had to have my prophesies translated into Greek. Very often after we received mail I would be greeted with cries like 'Hey Marconi! Is true my sister she marry just like you tell me'. I would have no idea what I had told them. In such a way I got to know first hand the social mode of Greek island life. For instance, matchmaking was still very much the order of the day and seamen often arranged matches by correspondance with other seamen. The dowry would run to serious money, for instance two thousand gold pounds or sovereigns was a starting bride price, which in those days was about six thousand pounds sterling. The Greeks didn't trust paper money as the government had a habit of devaluing the drachma by half overnight. They knew where they were with sovereigns which, minted in gold in Queen Victoria's time, could only increase in value.

Eventually we missed the charter for Karachi but secured one in Djibouti in French Somaliland. We were all heartily glad to be steaming down the Persian Gulf and leaving the suffocating heat engendered by a stationary ship. Work too has a social aspect, in that again I was in touch with other ships through the radio. I am reminded of the story of the Glasgow seaman's wife bemoaning her situation at home with her children. 'There's your feyther up the Persian Gulf enjoying hissel and yer puir auld mither sitting at haeme drinking cauld beer.'

SMALL CRISIS IN DJIBOUTI

We were to load salt at Djibouti for Japan and the charterers insisted we whitewash the hold for maximum cleanliness, but when we docked at Djibouti there were piles of rocksalt lying in the sun, with Somalis walking over it in their bare feet, and open to all the disease carrying bugs of Africa. The loading was done by half naked sweating Somalis shovelling the salt into balers which were swung over the hold and emptied. The Somalis are a tall, lean people, brown or black, and often with red hair and a curious red glow off their skin. Red haired black men are a bit incongruous but I noticed that the earth was also a red ochre colour so I suppose the food grown there was full of whatever chemical was in it. However they stood on the mountains of salt sweating copiously into what was destined for delicate Japanese stomachs.

Djibouti, now a state in its own right, was then a small colonial town with mostly mud or wooden houses and one imposing building in the shape of the post office. There was a little touch of France in an outdoor cafe, with a round advertising obelisk beside which squatted an elderly Negro in an old army greatcoat with medal ribbons and a tin labelled 'Mutilee de Guerre'. There were lots of French matelots about and thickset black soldiers from Senegal showing that the colony was of military importance, if no great shakes as a commercial centre. On the journey round from the Gulf I had experienced trouble with the H.F. transmitter and got round the problem by sending traffic to London via Aden and landline on the medium wave transmitter. Now came the moment of truth for me in my chosen profession. I would have to find the fault in the transmitter myself as there were no Marconi or other wireless company depots in Djibouti. The oceanspan transmitter had one large triode valve at the centre of its operations so I decided to replace it with the spare to see if that was the fault. Again no power at output. I replaced all the valves and still no change. Then I tested all the resistances coils and capacitors and indeed was unsure if they were giving correct readings or not. I worked in the heat every day trying to find the fault but without success. One is trained and indeed passes a test in fault finding but unless it is done every day it is not possible to build up a skill at this part of the job. I enlisted the help of an American R.O. who tested the triode with his spare one and we both gave a cheer when the power needle soared to maximum. Indeed, my spare triode was faulty and what must have happened was that a previous incumbent had changed the valve and put the dud one back in the spare locker. I breathed a silent curse on his incompetence. The Captain realized that I was doing my best and told me not to worry as we could make the short crossing to Aden where there was a Marconi depot. This would have cost the owners several thousand pounds in demurrage and lost time. It would have also black-balled me from future employment with the company, as I would be remembered as the Sparks who had cost them money, which to the Greek shipowner is unforgiveable. However the next problem to solve was where to get another triode? The Greek ship chandler came to the rescue at this point and by dint of the age old Greek custom of bribery, he secured a new triode from the French naval radio station. The same ship's chandler delivered five bags of flour that were completely black. White flour was delivered during the day and signed for but, under cover of darkness, a truck arrived and the black flour was swopped for the white. Why this elaborate charade was arranged was beyond me as we certainly knew we were eating black bread for the next three weeks. This reminds me of the story of the Greek ship that had slipped its moorings and was gliding out of the port of Philadelphia under cover of darkness in order to avoid paying the pilotage dues. The chief mate was out on the flying bridge checking that the ship was clear of the quay when the Captain hissed in a loud whisper, 'Come into the wheelhouse or they will see you'. How the port authorities could see the mate on the bridge and miss seeing a large vessel under way defeats my reasoning. Anyway, in such a way are fortunes made.

    The small Greek community in Djibouti would come down to the ship at night to converse with their fellow countrymen. The Greek word for fellow countryman is 'patriotis'. And the patriotis would sit on deck with members of the crew, drinking coffee and ouzo, sometimes singing taverna songs and if the spirit moved them, dancing to the music of the third engineer's guitar. One night one of the patriotis invited some of the officers out for a night on the town. I was invited to come with them, but as all the conversation was in Greek, I had no idea what they had in mind. We went first to the cafe on the square where we drank some excellent coffee and Couvoisier and then piled into the patriotis's Citroen and travelled some few miles along a dirt road to an unlit area of mud huts. The moment the Greek stopped the car it was surrounded by bare breasted Somali girls.

There were no men, black or white to be seen. The women were chattering like monkeys in their own language, but the international language of copulation was often on their lips. 'Vien Vien ! Ficky Ficky' they shrieked, accompanied by slapping motions of their two hands together. Our middle aged bald third engineer, rather like an overweight Kojack, sensibly wore a pith helmet for protection against the sun. One of the skinny black arms came into the car and removed the pith helmet. The exposure of Dimitri's bald head provoked shrieks of laughter and then a naked black breast was intruded into the car and rubbed over the bald pate. I watched as the semi-naked black women fell about shreiking and pointing. Poor Dimitri was embarrassed and not a little annoyed when the Greeks and the taxi driver joined in the laughter at his expense. I gathered from the absence of men that this was an African brothel in the bush and we must have been the first potential customers they had seen for some time. The going rate was the equivalent of five shillings which would have been a lot of money for a black man to find in those days. Anyway I sat down outside the hut in the moonlight while the others went in one after another to pay their respects to the ladies. As I lay against the side of the hut I was subjected to the other prostitutes pushing their bare breasts in my face repeating the erotic mantra 'vien ficky fick', the while. When my ship mates emerged they seemed satisfied but hardly elated and the subject of this commercial congress wasn't mentioned. The whole commercial aspect and loveless nature of the transaction repelled me, apart from the hazards of lack of hygiene, but the third engineer had no such reservations.'It's just the same bang to the orang-outang, as it is to your old dog Rover', he quoted from some previous sojourn on a British ship. Be that as it may, I contented myself with the lonely pleasures of the celibate.

  The next day, in a mood of self satisfaction, I went 'Up the road', which is the sailor's argot for going into the city centre as opposed to staying in the area of the docks. Eventually I found what would now be called a disco, but in those days would be known as a bar with a record player. The clientele were mostly French matelots with a few Swedish and Dutch merchant seamen. The women were all African, some of them very elegant in long multicoloured gowns. Unlike my West African experience I noticed they were all well shod, but they did not appear to be free agents, and I suspected a madam or a pimp or pimps lurking in the background. The music of Louis Armstrong and Count Basie crackled and hissed out from the record player. Like most people, I have always imagined that Africans had natural rhythm, but jazz was a non-starter for these girls. They just padded round the floor to their own seemingly internal beat, something like the half dance, half run, which we often see now on TV. The French matelots and the Swedes vainly tried to jive to the fast jazz rhythms but Louis Armstrong's music was too far ahead for the black ladies. I struck up a conversation with one of the Swedes, and like ourselves, they had been up the Gulf with cargo and had suffered appallingly from the heat with their fair complexions. The Dutchmen however had an air conditioning which was obligatory for any Dutch ship going into the Gulf. Even in those days the Dutch were far ahead in social legislation.

I noticed that one of the African girls was very much different from the others. She was about five foot nine inches tall, had a dark brown aquiline face, thin European lips and large almond shaped eyes and with long black eyelashes. She moved in a regal way, knowing full well her own worth in terms of physical beauty. I summoned up the courage to ask her to dance, taking care to keep my distance both for terpsichorean reasons and reasons of respect. I found out that she was an Abyssinian, could speak good English and appeared to be educated. The aspect of this night club was the same as most in the world, purely, venal. She was there to encourage the punters to drink bad alcohol at inflated prices. That was no problem as I was glad of her company and prepared to pay the inflated prices for the ill tasting French-African beer. Nature seemed to be taking its course but when I asked my charming companion for permission to escort her home, to my great surprise she refused. It was against the house rules she said, confirming my view that all the women were controlled. As it happened I had some cheap scarrib jewellery which I had bought off the bum boats in Port Said and as I carelessly laid them on the table I watched her almond eyes light up. 'We girls go together in a taxi', she said. 'Get another taxi, tell the driver to follow it and go into the house that I go into'. I waited with impatience for the bar to close, and like a 'B' movie actor from the films, I told the taxi driver 'Cette voiture la,' and as my French had run out 'Follow it'. Indeed the driver did follow the cab with the girls in it, to a residential area with modern bungalows with small gardens. 'La maison c'est la', said the driver pointing to a white bungalow on the corner. Receiving no reply to my knock, I turned the door handle and found the door unlocked so I entered. I thought it must have been a high class brothel or shebeen, but to my surprise I found myself in a well furnished bedroom with a black woman in the bed. She did not seem to be surprised to see me but did not speak or acknowledge my presence. It's got to be a brothel, I thought, and sat down on an upright chair against the wall. Someone is bound to come in if only to get money from me. Then a good looking young black man arrived, clad in vest and boxer shorts. He too ignored my presence and commenced to clean his teeth at the handbasin. I could see his face in the mirror. He was deliberately ignoring me. There was something in the way the man was cleaning his teeth which did not strike me as indicative of a man about to bed a strange woman. He looked as if he was performing a routine action untinged with any sense of urgency. In short, my instinct told me that the woman was his wife and that I was a trespasser in his house. I hurriedly left the room and looked at the other bungalows in the street. There were no lights in any of them, obviously the taxi man had made a mistake, and the beautiful Ethiopian girl was nowhere to be found. What the Somali couple thought about the strange white man sitting in their bedroom I don't know. I can only think that they thought that I was a French colonial policeman or some white man with really awesome authority. I would have loved to have been a fly on the wall to hear their conversation after I left.

    We sailed next morning with the H.F. transmitter working and our holds full of salt for Niigata in Japan, where hopefully further adventures would befall us.

SALT FOR NIIGATA

We sailed across the Indian Ocean with a side swipe from a hurricane that gave us three days and nights of storm tossed anxiety. One day the mate told me that the deck had disappeared under a huge wave and that before the ship could rise through the tons of water, a second wave crashed down on the deck. The gallant Okeanis managed to free herself from the water before the third wave crashed on the deck, otherwise she would have gone down. Several ships, including the huge bulk carrier 'Derbyshire', have disappeared without trace in this area, and I know I would not have been able to get a distress call away in such circumstances. The weather improved as it always does eventually, and we made our way down the Malacca Straits to the Indonesian island of Tanjong Ubang where we put in for bunkers. The reason for this call was that oil in Indonesia was cheap and the port officials were notoriously short sighted as far as Plimsole lines were concerned. This, the internationally approved line on every ship's hull, must always be visible above the water. Where oil is cheap it makes a saving of thousands of dollars to load the ship well above this line.

The harbour at Tanjong Ubang consists of a single jetty with an oil pipe so if I wanted to see something of Indonesia I had to go ashore to the nearest village. This was real Conrad country with dense jungle everywhere, but three-quarters of a mile of sandy road led to a well kept village of whitewashed huts with thatch roofs. A small group of brown skinned Indonesian youths posed for a photograph in front of a small statue of Joe Stalin, which seemed very incongruous in the jungle. As happens on these occasions, I was joined on the road by the ship's carpenter who spoke fair English and a moustachioed sailor from the islands who spoke only Greek. The carpenter was a cheerful veteran from the war years who told me he had gone adrift for two months in Poland at the end of the war. He had taken up with a Polish girl in Gydnia, missed his ship, and gone back with the girl to her village. Apparently he was treated with great kindness by the girl's parents and by the villagers, but all good things come to an end and he was repatriated to Greece. Although Iannis was a happy-go-lucky fellow without a political thought in his head he was followed everywhere by the Greek secret police until he found another ship.

We spotted a cafe there in the middle of a jungle village with a proud sign outside proclaiming the virtues of Guinness's stout. Armed with acceptable American dollars the chippy treated us both to bottles of Guinness's glutinous stout which the sailor was unable to finish and opted instead for Malayan Tiger beer. Having a love and respect for the Polish people in common, the chippy and I reminisced about times ashore in Gydnia and Gdansk while the potent Guinness went straight to his head. He railed against the greedy bloodsucking Greek shipowners, waved his dollars aloft and called for more drinks, every time I suggested we get back on board. Meantime the monoglut sailor had disappeared, presumably returning to the ship. Eventually the sailor reappeared on a bicycle with word from the Captain to return to the ship as it was ready to sail. By this time the carpenter was footless and like Rab. C. Nesbitt, shouting defiance to the wind and announcing that he was going to stay in Indonesia like he did in Poland. The sailor indicated that I was to return alone if the chippy was still impervious to reason. Then I had the bright idea to suggest that we buy some Guinness to bring back to the ship where we could continue the party. This idea met with the carpenter's approval so we set off in fine style, in a rickshaw, with the sailor bringing up the rear on his bicycle. We trundled along the jungle road, the chippy roaring his head of about God knows what in Greek and clutching his dozen stout.

The Captain and the Indonesian pilot stood on the flying bridge, the crew lined the rail, while the fore and aft deck parties stood by the mooring ropes. Iannis, the carpenter, still shouting defiance to the world at large and clutching his dozen stout to his chest, mounted the gangway while I followed shamefacedly behind and went straight to the radio room. Once on board, the chippy straightened up, ceased shouting, and, as if assuming again the status and discipline of a petty officer, went staight to his station for'ard at the anchor winch and carried out his duties without a word. There were no recriminations from the Captain who I think was quite pleased that I refused to abandon the carpenter and brought him safely back on board. It is rare to see a drunken Greek, as drunkeness in Greece is considered a social disgrace. When they do get drunk it is usually for reasons of inner tension or deep unhappiness and tends to invoke a response of pity. Anyway, the strong Guinness had crept up on our chippy and we had a good laugh at it on the slow journey up to Japan.

Passing the coast of Formosa, without warning, a propellar driven plane swooped out of the clouds and swept low over our ship. I could see the oriental pilot's face as he looked out of his cockpit to observe us. I thought he was going to strafe our ship with machine gun fire and we were all thoroughly frightened. It all happened so quickly that it was impossible to take cover in time but luckily nothing untoward happened and his mission was probably to take note of our name and course to report to the Americans who had a trade embargo on China at the time.

Later on that night I had a telegram to send to London which would usually be routed through Singapore, but this time I was able to raise Portishead radio direct and clear my message in a few minutes. The oceanspan transmitter is normally only good for three thousand miles but on this occasion I managed to transmit over a record distance of eight thousand miles and I was very proud to tell the operator at Portishead I was reaching him from the coast of Taiwan. The ability to maintain and operate a radio station at peak efficiency was a source of pride to me but unfortunately my achievement meant little to the others who had only a very hazy notion of what I was about.

We entered the area between Korea and Japan and were a day's steaming from Niigata when, transfixed as a rabbit in a car headlight, I watched a mine float by at a distance of twenty feet from the ship. At this time the Korean war had only been over about two years and this was probably a floating straggler from that conflict. The second mate who was on watch should have seen it, but no doubt he was painting and chipping instead of keeping a proper lookout. Dimitrios Koutsoukis was the second mate, a native of Andros, and of an indeterminate age between seventy and eighty. He had been at sea all his life mainly with the rank of bosun, but because of his experience he was promoted second mate although he had absolutely no knowledge of navigation. He couldn't bear to be idle and spent his time on watch chipping and painting the metal work on the bridge.

The tendency on Greek ships was to cut the officer strength to the bare minimum required by the international law, so that on our ship the only qualified navigating officers were the Captain and chief officer. As I write deregulation is the order of the day which has had the effect of letting British and Norwegian shipowners operate under flags of convenience, and in the interest of fatter profits, do without the services of qualified navigators and radio officers, using satellite navigation and communications. However this is false economy as when these systems break down there is no way of summoning help in an emergency. I reported the mine sighting to the Captain who gave me a position to report to the Japanese coast authorities. My warning was being broadcast by all the Japanese coast stations within fifteen minutes, proof, if proof were needed, of life at sea being made safer by a radio officer on board.

A day later we docked at Niigata, a port unknown to even old Stamatis, our Liverpool, Burmese, Greek speaking Indian, who had been everywhere. This was in the time before the Japanese economic explosion, when Japan was still regarded as a cheap labour country, good at copying western goods but not very good at quality or originality. Approaching the entrance to Niigata harbour in the lee of Sado island I felt the excitement of the explorer by sea, which I have always felt when visiting a country for the first time. After three weeks at sea the first landfall, the first sight of the pilot boat, the first sight of the Japanese faces of its crew, the strange uniform of the pilot, all these trigger off a euphoria that to me justifies the boredom of the long days at sea. We docked at the outer harbour to find a small lorry on the quayside filled with crates of beer. An important looking Japanese with a retinue of factotums, followed at a respectful distance by a beautiful kimono clad girl, boarded our ship. Captain Samothrakis, unshaven and wearing his jeans and sweatshirt, was immediately suspicious. 'I never ordered all this stuff', he said to the important looking Japanese. Indeed we were all pretty scruffy as the weather had been bad making it difficult to do the washing and ironing and the ship was caked with salt and streaked with rust. Chief Officer Spiros at least had on his German officer's cap although he had a day's stubble. There was much bowing and scraping by the Japanese and in the course of the exchanges I gathered that we were the first foreign ship to grace the port of Niigata since before World War II.

The important looking man turned out to be the mayor of Niigata and the beautiful girl in the kimono was the beauty queen. The Captain grudgingly welcomed them on board but he was still suspicious of their intent; Greeks bearing gifts in reverse as it were. Reporters and photographers were on hand to record our every utterance and it was then that I gathered that the lorry load of beer was for our crew and there was a crate of whiskey for the officers. As far as I can remember it was all put into stores and issued sparingly on Greek Orthodox saint days. It is doubtful if our scruffy images did anything to enhance the commerce of the port. Next, health inspectors in white coats and masks crawled all over our salt cargo blissfully unaware of the vast quantities of Somali loincloth sweat it had absorbed during loading. The immigration officials interviewed us individually, and just as you thought, from the blanked yellow visages, that you were going to be declared an undesirable alien, the official, straight out of central casting, handed you a map of Niigata with the brothel areas marked in red and euphemistically labelled amusement areas.

This was the first port since leaving Manchester that could be described as developed, so there was much care taken by the Greeks in their toilet preparations. Wedding rings were removed and tossed in drawers, toilet water and hair oil liberally applied and collars and ties worn for the first time in months. The agents had supplied a free standby taxi for the use of the Captain, and as he only went ashore on ship's business he allowed me to use it. I think it was in his nature to extract the maximum value from all his perks, whether he could make use of them himself or not. He was a dour, uncommunicative man who had seen it all. He was supremely cynical about rapacious shipowners and lazy sailors alike. I found out later that most of the Greek captains were like Samothrakis, isolating themselves in their cabins, dining alone in a saloon meant for twelve, as if they could not trust themselves to be gregarious, which all Greeks naturally are. At times Captain Samothrakis would come to the after rail of the bridge and taunt and harangue the crew. I have very little idea what the subject of the taunts were, but I suspect that it had to do with the Athens/Ionian islands rivalry which was a good humoured source of banter on all the Goulandris ships. One day I called at the Captain's quarters and found him playing with a toy train he had bought in Niigata for his son. The toy was well worn by the time we got to Cardiff!

Thirty yearts later I was to phone Captain Samothrakis in Cardiff and was answered by the same son who was now a radio officer sailing on the Greek ships and speaking English with a resonant and cultured accent. The Captain had eventually retired to Athens with his Welsh wife, but the pollution and heat proved too much for them, so they returned to Cardiff for the evening of their lives, a city of beauty and culture to match any in Europe.

Niigata city was like a toytown. Higgledy-piggledy houses, shops, and bars decked with neon signs in Japanese characters crowded up against each other giving the impression that space was fast running out for Japan. Being six foot two inches tall and sporting a Van Dyke beard, I made an incongruous sight in my tweed sports coat and flannels, compared with the smooth faced short Japanese who all seemed to dress in kimonos and wooden shoes. People came out of shops and bars to look at the hairy giant. Those days are alas long gone with innocence in this age of quick and easy travel, of electronic images that sweep the globe from one end to the other. Some of the bars were smaller than my granny's kitchen, but they held six bar stools and often two doll-like girls in kimonos. The chief mate and second engineer accompanied me into a bar where there was room for us all to sit down. Immediately we were joined by three young doll-like girls in kimonos. Apparently their function was to serve as a poor man's geisha; that is to make polite conversation, pour the customer's drink and mop the customer's brow when necessary. Their boss was known as the Mama-San to whom all requests for pass outs had to be directed. I suppose they performed the same function as hostesses in a West End club, but in a much more civilized way. There the similarity ended as they did not order expensive drinks, and they did not drink coloured water and pretend it was champagne. All in all, their manner was courteous, and they made it appear that their customer's good humour was the most important matter on their mind. They were delighted to know that we were not Americans, whom they regarded as loud and insensitive, but they had only a vague idea where Britain was and had never heard of Greece. Three affection-starved males were made to feel the most important people in the world and if the girls were acting they did it well.

    We left the bar and found ourselves in a building with the legend 'dancing' written in neon over the door. This proved to be a night club full of Americans, both black and white. The local girls there had forsaken the kimono for jeans and check shirts and I noticed that some of them had curiously round eyes. I found out later that some Japanese women underwent operations to have their eyelids slit to make them more European looking. Looking round the club with its American airmen dressed in the shore going uniform of baseball hats, jeans and Hawaiin shirts, I realised that two cultures were mixing here and the American one, so different in all its aspects, was to be the dominant one.

    A tall, louche American overheard me speaking English to the Greeks and enquired about my accent. Glad to speak English again with a native speaker, I introduced him to my Greek companions and explained our presence in Japan, while he gave us some sound advice about what to do and see in Niigata. I was receiving regular mail from Poland, some in Polish, some in German, which followed me round the world and I talked about Poland to our new American friend who was a civilian technician attached to the American Air Force. We forgot about the friendly American when we 'clicked', as they say in Ulster. The two ladies escorted us to their house and we also lost the Chief Mate at some time in the night. Needless to say, our stay in Japan was devoted to a headlong dash to hedonism, which is understandable due to the lack of female company, entertainment, and indeed any form of social existence at sea. Our American friend managed to meet up with us every night we were ashore, joining us for drinks in the delightful bar with the geisha girls and the Mama-San.

Four months later when I joined a ship in Philadelphia, I received a letter from the American, posted in Philadelphia, and stating that he had gone there to study at the university. Of course I phoned him, marvelling at the coincidence of my going there at the same time as himself and we met for a drink. It was not until decades later when revelations about the C.I.A. began to be published that I realised that his interest was probably connected with the letters from Poland that I was getting and that his arrival in Philadelphia was no mere coincidence.

Anyway, at the time my thoughts were far from C.I.A. agents and espionage but I remember the second engineer and myself being in deep culture shock when we entered a Japanese house for the first time. The walls, floor and ceiling were wooden, highly polished and spotlessly clean, the door was a paper sliding one, and the furniture consisted of a long low coffee table. The bedroom, no more than seven feet square, contained a thin mattress and a sheet. The only departure from wood and paper was a concrete bath tub in the bathroom. It was three feet deep, smooth and sunken, reminding me of sheep dips I had seen in the Mourne mountains. We were asked to remove our shoes when entering, to protect the delicate polished surface of the floor. This would be a custom the west would do well to emulate.

A curious ritual with the bathtub followed, requiring us to strip off and immerse ourselves in the tub. Dimitri bridled at this, the implication being that he could do with a bath, though the real reason was that most Greeks have in innate sense of modesty. He resented displaying his body before two strange ladies and another man, even though no doubt he had rather closer intimacies in mind for the young lady. However, I found it a delightfully sensual experience to be immersed in water up to my chest with tiny Japanese hands busy with the shampoo and massage. Next we were rubbed down with warm towels and led away for discussions of a not entirely Japanese nature. Second engineer Dimitri was required to be on board in the morning to supervise the maintainance of the engines, but, as the radio station was closed down by international law while in port, I was as free as a bird. A taxi to the dockside with the two westernised ladies brought a chorus of Japanese hisses from the dockers, but the two ladies undeterred by this, came on board.

This reaction is now called racism, is greatly deplored, and regarded as very unsophisticated, but I think it is a fundamental instinct of the male of the species to resent the bedding of its females by a male of another tribe. There is of course a high degree of nationalism imbedded in the Japanese psyche which developed in isolation from the rest of the world. The contempt that the Japanese feel for the lesser breeds manifested itself one time when my companion and I passed a section of the city inhabited by Koreans. She spoke of them with unconcealed contempt although for all the world they looked the same as Japanese to me, but, as I write, petty little nationalisms are tearing Europe apart, not least in my own country. The fanaticism and cruelty of the Japanese in the second world war, which at one time made them seem invincible, was due mainly to their view of themselves as culturally and spiritually superior to the west. One of the benefits of the self imposed isolation of Captain Samothrakis was his non-interference with the day to day running of the ship. We brought our visitors on board quite openly while the chief steward prepared and served a breakfast for us. Our consorts were horrified at the dirt of our accommodation and my lady insisted on washing the wash-hand basin before she would use it although it was cleaned every day by the steward.

On an iron decked ship, the deck is soaked regulary with fish oil to guard against rust, and the fish oil is tramped through the carpets in the accommodation. On British ships there is a practice of tying a rope around the cabin carpet, lashing it to the deck rail and throwing the carpet into the sea to be dragged in the ship's wake for an hour. This I did regularly but the next application of fish oil would stain it again. After the sparse cleanliness of a Japanese house our ship must have seemed a floating slum.

Some of the sailors had brought on board bar girls from the quaintly named amusement area just outside the dock gates. What they thought of the stygian squalor of the eight man cabins, God only knows. The all male milieu of the merchant ship on long trips is a deterrent to decent standards, both mentally and physically. Later when I was to work on a Norwegian ship I was happily surprised to find some women crew members and a resulting pride in appearance and elevation of standards of speech and conversation.

The next twenty-four hours were spent on meals in restaurants, visits to Shinto shrines, watching colourful Samurai figures parade through the city in what appeared to be a manifestation of xenophobia. Frequent returnings to the ship for replenishment of funds established a glorious ritual of recreation, excitement, and the sweet satisfaction of deep dreamless sleep of complete fulfillment. When we saw a film set first in Ireland, I explained to my companion that this was the island from which I hailed, but the film swiftly changed to a location in South Africa and she became even more confused.

My companion was quick, intelligent, quite beautiful, and, I am sure whatever course her life would take, she was one of life's survivors. One who, having put herself outside of Japanese society, would sniff out the best bet in the options open to her in western society. I think of her married to some American officer and living the life of an American matriarch in California. My money had run out, so we returned to the ship to get a sub, but unfortunately the agent apparently had a cashflow problem and no Japanese currency was to be had. My girl had obviously heard such a story before, so she made her excuses and left, never to be seen again. Of course it was par for the course and to be expected, but none the less I felt the ache in the heart that tells us that man was not meant to live alone.

Meanwhile the cargo was rapidly being unloaded, the crew spending most of their time at the 'amusement area' outside the dock gates. Walking through the crew's accommodation one day, I passed the showers where two young deck apprentices were dancing 'a ring a rosie' under the spray with two equally young hostesses. Apparently they had fallen in love and had not left the ship for three days. All over the ship Venus was sporting with Neptune. A family of Japanese traders set up their stall on the midships hatch cover displaying mass produced wooden Shinto shrine miniatures, hollowed out bamboo sticks with Japanese characters carved on them and various other tourist kitch now seen in every airport duty-free shop. Their daughter, a pretty child of about thirteen or fourteen had found a way to augment her pocket money by offering sex to the crew.

One by one, in the coming weeks, those unfortunates who had availed of her tender delights made their way to the mate's office with weeping penises. The Chief Officer would give them shots of penicillin to dry up the discharge and later when we docked in Canada they would go to the hospital for medical examinations. Today, with the killer Aids virus which is endemic in certain parts of the world, it is frightening to think of what could happen in such a situation.

A walk in the countryside revealed a fairytale landscape, with fields cultivated to the very edge of the road. Not an inch of land was wasted, no hedges or ditches anywhere. Cherry blossoms, neat wooden houses with an Alpine backdrop gave the impression of being in another world. In those days there were not many cars so one's reverie was only broken by the odd cyclist or a passing bus. Cameras were then the product where these ingenious people had surpassed the world in quality so we all bought them. The married men amongst us bought marvellous mechanical toys to present to their children, at a cost of roughly half the price obtaining in Europe. Later on the Japanese, with their relentless worship of work, were to outstrip the west in most fields of human endeavour except quality of life. Of course once the western goods were outpriced, the Japanese could dominate the market as in the case of motor bikes where only one British factory remains. As I write, East European factories are being closed as 'uneconomic' and one can be sure the void will be filled with Japanese goods.

A night ashore at the 'Mama Sans' bar ended in a party in the ship's saloon by kind permission of the Captain and indeed it was a very civilised affair with Greek coffee and ouzo. Next evening at sundown we sailed for Canada and as the dockers threw off the ropes a taxi drew up on the quay. Four dainty figures in kimonos emerged bearing bouquets of flowers. In a touching scene they lined the dock throwing flowers at the departing ship as tears streamed down their delicate doll-like faces. We waved fom the rails until the dockside merged in the gathering dusk. By way of response it was agreed that we send a telegram of thanks and farewell. It seems that these bar girls were greatly moved by the way they were treated by the Greeks. The Greeks offered them little presents, valued their affections, and generally showed them repect as human beings. I had seen middle aged Japanese businessmen in their cups, tired and bad tempered after a day in the office, treat these girls as if they were bondslaves. The girls were obliged to be polite even when they were humiliated and insulted. One could see the hurt in their young eyes at the gratuitous abuse offered to them. Well, like a scene from H.M.S. Pinafore, we quit the shores of Japan, headed north through the straits of Tsugar and out into the North Pacific.

For the first time since taking over the Okeanis, the Greek shipowner in Paris had not found a cargo near at hand, so we had to sail to Vancouver in Western Canada where a cargo of timber had been found to ship to Cardiff. The northern route heading towards the Arctic circle was the shortest way, so we ploughed through stormy seas in almost permament darkness and in bitter cold. For two weeks everyone was miserable, and, as I remember it, I stayed near a radiator for most of the time I was off watch. There was no radio traffic the whole way across until we approached the Alaskan coast when the low power coast station at Kodiak came into earshot. Then we headed south down the coast of British Columbia into the Juan da Fuca Straits when we docked one morning at New Westminster.

M.V. Okeanis, Niigata, Japan

Japanese traders on deck of M.V. Okeanis

DEEP IN THE CANADIAN WOODS

The impressively clean Frazer River rushes through this small port situated on the outskirts of Vancouver where the snow topped Rockies descend into the autumn forests of the coastal foothills, vying for sky space with the skyscrapers of the city.The bad weather darkness and gloom had lasted right up to the previous night. Now we basked in warm autumn sunshine alongside a lumber wharf with the usual bustle of customs men and immigration officials with their strange uniforms and strange accents. The Canadian accent, delivered in forthright measured tones, is pleasant and only differs from the American in its pronounciation of the 'ou' sound, which is pronounced rather like the west of England accent as in 'doubt'. Perhaps it was culture shock, but to me the Canadians seemed rather uncouth after mixing with the over polite Japanese. Their officials were officious, and later I found that this was the case all over North America. For instance, we had a non-English-speaking crew but no Canadian ever prefaced his conversation with 'Do you speak English?' I believe this impoliteness sprang from the hostility to immigrants who could not speak English and threatened the native-born Canadians' job security. No one seemed surprised that I spoke English better than they did, presuming I suppose that I was better educated than the rest. One of the first Canadians up the gangplank after we docked was a Jehovah's Witness about his business of proselytising. His wife was from County Antrim and he recognised my accent straight away. You will realise that to show any interest whatever in religion in these circumstances is fatal, so I escaped by showing him the sailors mess and assuring him that the Greek seamen discussed little else but religion. Again the imperious assumption was made that the sailors one and all spoke English. Our Ionian Islanders sat bemused and respectful as the Jehovah's Witness harangued them on the coming of the Lord. Eventually Fat Petros tumbled to the fact that he was an evangelist and not an immigration official threatening them with confinement to the ship.Fat Petros rose to his feet with a slow growl of disgust. 'Gamutta Panayia', he exploded, which is a common Greek expression meaning roughly, 'Fuck the Virgin Mary.' The dozen or so other sailors fell about laughing when I explained the nature of the harangue to which they had listened for half an hour.

New Westminster had neat rows of wooden houses, mostly alike, with well kept but uninspiring gardens. At night the boring main street was ablaze with neon signs, sometimes misspelt, such as 'Busses' on a bus station. The bars, I discovered, sold only cold beer served with salt, a custom apparently peculiar to the west coast of Canada. To get the atmosphere of the place I searched the local paper in vain. Work I gather was scarce, pay was better across the border in the U.S. where prices were also lower. In vain I searched the main street at night for somewhere to go but all I could see were people waiting for a bus home or youths cruising the streets aimlessly in huge American cars obviously as bored as I was. There was however a Flying Angel Club, that last refuge of the bored and impecunious seaman. I did however meet a politically educated Canadian docker on board. I gather he was a Communist but in those days it was dangerous to say so openly. He told me about the unemployment camps in Canada in the thirties, when single men were herded together in the mountains to cut timber and repair roads. He told me the party was well organized in these camps and staged strikes which caused the government to take fright and closed them down. This interesting worker also told me he was deported from Boston for organising Canadian immigrant workers there.

One evening I went to a dance I had seen advertised in the local paper taking two Greek sailors with me. The Canadian girls refused point blank to dance with the Greeks and when we saw a twenty stone youth casually bang the head of another youth against a pillar we became alarmed. While this was going on the partners of the two boys stared into the middle distance casually chewing gum. We decided to go back to the ship.

After Japan everything in Canada seemed larger than life. Huge cars, six lane highways skirted by supermarkets, surrounded by acres of car parking space, presaged the developments to come two decades later in Europe. Land of course is plentiful and cheap in Canada but the other side of the coin is frightful: urban sprawl and the dead city heart that characterises so many North American cities. New York is the one exception of which I know, Time Square with all its tattiness, seeming to be the centre of the universe. Los Angeles, which I have surveyed from the sea, is the end product of this lack of planning, with its 200 miles of polluted ugliness. Vancouver itself has a majestic setting, the skyscrapers reaching for the clouds as if in competition to the magnificent Rockies ringing the city.

There is a very fine park in central Vancouver sloping down to the sea, with dozens of examples of North American flora on display. A school pal of mine had emigrated to Vancouver by virtue of a tranfer from the Belfast office of the Commercial Union Insurance Co. I telephoned him and within minutes I was on my way to his mother's house in the suburbs. The whole family had emigrated with him and although I could see that they were homesick they were making the best of it. The mother, who used to own Harrison's paper shop on the Cregagh Road, missed the conviviality of the customers and the general friendship of Belfast. Her second husband, an ex Royal Ulster Rifleman, had followed her out. He had no trade, due to service in the army, but had managed to get a job in Eaton's warehouse. Eaton's, the biggest chain store in Canada, was founded by an Ulsterman but apparently with no thought then of ethnic discrimination legislation. Ulstermen were proudly given preferment. In this happy environment Mrs Harrison's husband was happy if not rich. Mrs Harrison made a batch of Ulster potato bread for me to bring back to the ship and after showing the cook how to fry it I watched with quiet amusement as my bemused mess mates contemplated their strange breakfast. They ate the bread with relish when I explained to them that this was our national dish. Later on in the voyage the steward found a case of H.P. sauce buried in the store room, a legacy from the previous British owners. This too, to my surprise, the Greeks ate with relish. Those sophisticated travellers to Corfu and the like, who wince on hearing the packaged holidaying Brits demand their brown sauce in the taverna would do well to note this.

    Half a day's trip across the bay brought us to Victoria on Vancouver Island, the most English of cities in Canada. The impressive Parliament Buildings in classical style reminded me of the Belfast city hall but there the resemblance ceased. Sedate lawn fronted villas and cherry blossom gave a whiff of Cheltenham with a dash of Portsmouth, added by the presence of matelots of the Royal Canadian Navy outfitted with traditional bellbottoms and Nelson's ribbons.

    A day later we moved up Vancouver Sound with densely wooded mountains looming up on either side. The stillness of the atmosphere plus the smell of rotting wood is my abiding memory of this curious corner of the world. The rotting smell is caused by millions of logs floated down the rivers to the waters of Vancouver Straits where they are marshalled by tugs into the yards of the sawmills.

The small logging town of Nanaimo was our last loading port where we were loaded with timber boards right up to the bottom of the funnel. Nanaimo was a wooden bungalowed village with supermarket, post office, a bank and several uninspiring beer parlours. Although the scenery was as grand as anything in the highlands of Scotland alas there is an air of remoteness and terminal boredom. Some immigrants from Greece drove over from another village to talk to our crew. They had a large American car, were obviously hard working and had prospered. However the emptiness of their lives in Canada was illustrated by the fact that a trip to talk to the crew of a Greek ship was a high point in their lives.

Loaded to the gunnels with pine boards, the Okeanis dodged out of Juan de Fuca Straits to the broad Pacific to meet a raging gale. Without hesitation our Captain turned the ship round into the sheltered waters of the Straits until the storm abated. Many captains, fearful of delays and consequential reprimands from the owners, would have ploughed on at reduced speed, causing danger and discomfort to the crew, but Samothrakis was his own man and took decisions without discussing the options with anyone. In later years when I became the owner/skipper of a fishing vessel I followed his example.

The weather abated and so we headed down the Pacific coast of North America. It got warmer and the skies got blue, as did the gentle Pacific swell, and the prospect of the trip to Britain lifted everyone's spirits. Singsongs would take place on the fantail at the heel of the evening and I can still sing a verse or two of Apopse Fillame, a melancholy Greek sailors song.

Boinnggg!!! The noise of the ship's foghorn had me out of bed at 6am. A foghorn has the same effect as the sound of the air-raid sirens during the war, a warning of impending doom. I looked out and could only see as far as the ship's rail. It was a real Californian pea souper caused by the range of temperatures plus the Los Angeles pollution.

To be ready for any emergency I switched on the main receiver and started the generator to power the main transmitter. The next thing I heard was a whirring sound as an artillery shell passed between the masts. At the end of the next silence period on 500 kcs, Oakland radio put out a navigational warning about coastal artillery practise in the region. The Captain was on the bridge when I brought the message. His response was a torrent of abuse in Greek as he telegraphed full speed ahead to get out of the firing area. Then we heard what every seaman fears the most, the sound of breakers on the shore. We pulled round 60 degrees and headed out to sea, away from the shore, and hopefully out of the range of the coast artillery.

An hour later we were basking in Californian sunshine as we made harbour at San Pedro. San Pedro is one of the myriad suburbs of Los Angeles which spreads along the Californian coastline for about 20 miles. As far as the eye can see the white bungalows spread over the nearby hills and out to the mountains on the distant horizon. The harbour at San Pedro serves as a naval base, with slick grey warships in serried ranks along the wharfs and our overladen timber boat was moored in the middle like the spectre at the feast. Our bunkering barge arrived and having an opportunity to go ashore for an hour with the agents launch, I dipped my toe in Uncle Sam's waters for the first time.

First impressions of California were exciting. Spanish colonial architecture, palm trees, bright colours and people of all races all add up to an atmospheric scene which perhaps explains why California has been a magnet, attracting people from all over the world. A visit to the men's store was made to purchase what was then the badge of the sophisticate in Ulster, a Yankee shirt with a button down collar. The shop assistant, a well dressed man in his fifties, broke into a huge grin on hearing my request. 'My God! That's the first time I have heard that accent in thirty-five years! You're from Northern Ireland, right?' He then told me he had served in the U.S. Navy in Londonderry during the first world war and had driven a Navy truck over the Glenshane Pass to Belfast. I really made that man's day! I suppose that Northern Ireland was not on everybody's lips in Los Angeles and to be reminded of one's youth is always welcome.

Shirt purchased, I returned on board to discover the immigration service quizzing the crew in the saloon. At that time two inglorious Irish-Americans, Senators McCarthy and MacCarron, had introduced a law that required visitors and seamen to submit to a political vetting before setting foot in the United States. The MacCarron Act forbad anyone who had ever been a member of the Communist Party from entering the country. I kept quiet about my quick trip ashore and watched the immigration men quiz the three sailors who needed to see a doctor. None of the seamen spoke English but that didn't deter the immigration men from asking all their questions in English. 'Communistas oiche?' I said to fat Petros who nodded vigorously.

The immigration man, realizing that he had been wasting his time, proceeded to fill in the form from his own observations. He held back fat Petros's eyelid to determine the colour of his eyes. Petros presumed that the immigration man must have been the doctor and protested vigorously in Greek that his eyes were O.K. and that it was his stomach that was bothering him. When I translated, the whole assembly collapsed with laughter.

The MacCarron Act was greatly resented by the seamen and there were quite a few Greek seamen who had been members of the Communist resistance who were barred from shore leave in the U.S. The immigration did not just take your word for the fact that you had never joined the party but consulted a huge tome that held thousands of names. For myself, I had given critical support to the party but never joined due to my revulsion at the show trials both before and after the war. I knew, as did everybody at the time who thought about it, that we owed our very existence to the heroism of the Red Army under the leadership of Joe Stalin, as they had faced 380 axis divisions against 180 faced by Eisenhower. The show trials stuck in my craw and I could not defend them as I would be obliged to do as a party member. I still resented having to conform to a backward bastard like MacCarron's world view, before going ashore.

One of the Greeks who had been an officer in the Greek army fighting the Communists in the Greek civil war, found, to his dismay, that his name was in the immigration's big book. He had the very common Greek name of Christos Christodoulis, a Greek equivalent of John Smith. A party member with the same name, from the same town, was there in the book so poor Christos was banned from shore leave in U.S. ports. As the ship was trading between the U.S. mainland and Puerto Rico, a U.S. colony, he was confined to the ship for 6 months. Eventually the Greek ambassador in Washington got him a D2, as the shore pass was called. At the time the entire crew of the French liner Normandy refused to answer the political questions of the U.S. immigration and this created some hysteria in the U.S. I learned later that the Normandy's crew were mostly right wing Corsicans who bitterly resented this intolerable intrusion into their private opinions. There was an American seaman in SanFrancisco, who, when hauled in front of the McCarthy inquisition, replied to every question, 'It's none of your damned business'. That man is the true stuff of moral courage and should have a statue raised to him.

At the same time blood-stained Irish ex-terrorists were being admitted to the U.S. without let or hindrance.

We left San Pedro and headed south, down the Mexican coast to the aptly named Panamanian town of Colon at the entrance to the Panama Canal. We were on the last lap of our journey round the world and heading to what was home for me, but just another foreign country to the Greeks. We received mail at Colon, amongst which was a letter for one Ioannis, a fireman who lived with a woman in Cardiff. As Ioannis could read neither Greek nor English he asked me to read the letter from his Welsh partner. Ioannis was in his forties, tough and cunning, and had the reputation of being a hard man, handy both with the fists and a knife. The Captain, also a Cardiff resident, had an affinity with him and told me he sent a regular allotment to his Welsh woman. I glanced down the letter to get the gist of it before I read it out. Indeed there was cause for caution, for the woman was basically dumping him, but also announcing that she had been living with a Maltese man for the past six months. She regretted, she wrote, that she had not informed him before but she feared that he would stop the allotment and, as the Maltese found difficulty getting out of bed in the morning to go to work, she needed the money for living expenses. Needless to say I broke the news as gently as I could and left out the bit about the lazy Maltese lover. Ioannis went white, his dark eyes flashed and he emitted a string of ferocious Greek oaths. 'I will keel her', he said and I believed him. The engineers believed him too and tried to talk him out of it. A telegram was dispatched to the shipping office cancelling his allotment but the captain was also worried that he would murder the woman when we got to Cardiff. When we did get to Cardiff he did not even bother to go to see her, but lived on board instead, which in the circumstances was just as well.

Moving up the Canal, as wondrous as ever, passing ships of all sizes, shapes and nationalities, we docked at Christobal. I went ashore with the Chief Officer and who should tag along with us but the carpenter who had caused the delay in Indonesia, as cheerful as ever. We stopped at the night club where I had made my shore leave debut as a trainee on the Port Napier. In broad tropical daylight it looked tawdry and unexciting. The proprietor, as it happened, arrived just at that time and turned out to be a 'Patriotis' - a fellow Greek. 'Patriotis ihnne', the magic words opened up a torrent of Hellenic conversation between the three of them, and the upshot of it was a flurry of telephone calls to the artists who were requested to turn up and put on a private show. Apparently the mate had a hundred dollars obtained from the stevedores as a tip, and was prepared to pay whatever was necessary. About six mulatto girls arrived within ten minutes and the cabaret began. Devoid of live music, the girls did their best to create an atmosphere, dancing with us, sitting on our knees and lowering drinks as fast as they could. One of them was white and the rest were a mixture of Spanish, Indian and Negro which is typical for Panama and accounts for much of the exotic nature of that country. Patriotis or not, the Greek proprietor milked the chief of every last dollar which was no mean feat in those days. This time, however, we were back on board on time and were soon ploughing through the Caribbean on our way to Cardiff.

WELSH RAREBITS

After an uneventful passage across the western ocean we finally reached the Bristol Channel and Cardiff roads. Cardiff, once the centre of the huge coal export trade, now languished as a run down and half empty port with derelict wharves. No sooner were the ropes ashore when a lorry drew up alongside, the winch was started up and wooden huts, ladders, dog kennels and all manner of wooden artefracts were unloaded and transferred to the lorry which drove off at high speed. The Captain, taking advantage of a limitless supply of Canadian pine, had the carpenter make him everything that could be made of wood that he thought would be useful at his home. The carpenter, who ranked as a petty officer, did not really have enough work about the ship to keep him busy so this was a useful way to employ his skills without loss to anyone except perhaps the timber importer who counted his cargo in millions of cubic feet. The lorry was well away before the customs came aboard and for me the familiar British uniform was a welcome sight.

My first trip ashore was to the Radio Officers' Union were I paid my nine months back 'subs' and endeavoured to find out something about union meetings. The area official was not available but from the personable girl assistant I was able to discern that the union democracy was moribund and no meetings actually took place. This young woman was the first attractive female I had seen for many weeks so I immediately asked her out only to hear her say in her charming Welsh lilt that she was really very small. At that she stood up behind her desk, and indeed she was only about 4 foot 10. As I am 6 foot 2 inches I was very embarrassed but what could I say. I could have said, 'O.K. the date is off, you are indeed a midget', or any other form of words which would have conveyed the same thing and made my excuses and left. But no, I had to say, 'That is not important', knowing that the whole arrangement would be a disaster, as indeed it turned out to be.

We decided to visit the cinema which was painless enough, but walking down past the Castle who should we pass but four of my shipmates walking abreast towards us. I watched them struggle to conceal their mirth at the incongruous sight we must have made. I left the young lady to the bus for the valleys and returned to the ship in the Bute Street area. This area is known as the Tiger Bay, and at that time consisted of Victorian back-to-back houses, smoke blackened and semi derelict. The inhabitants were mostly half castes, descendants of African and Arab seamen and their mostly common law wives. Many of these seamen were Moslems, as indeed the ones I sailed with on the Ravenspoint were, and had wives and families in their own countries. However it was an interesting social experience to sit in a bar and watch the brown and off-white people speak with broad Welsh accents about football and cricket, josh with the prostitutes of all colours who came in and out, supping ale in a setting that was as British as the Chelsea pensioners' home. These were the days before mass immigration from the West Indies and India changed the whole social fabric of Britain's inner cities.

We finished discharging in Cardiff and a short dodge up the Irish Sea brought us to the port of Liverpool where I had decided to pay off. The mates and engineers asked me to stay on but I knew that I had not been getting the full market rate for the job and was determined to put a higher price on my services to the next shipowner. I was sorry to leave the Okeanis as I felt appreciated there and had formed friendships with many of the crew.

With nine months' pay in my pocket I made my farewells and hopped aboard the Belfast ferry to spend Christmas in my native city. The familiar Ulster accents of the ferry crew were music to my ears, though for the first time in my seafaring career I felt a pang about leaving a ship that had been my home for nine months.

This time home my father had remarried, so I had made arrangements to stay with an aunt on the south side of the city. Little had changed in my absence and indeed Belfast in the fifties seemed moribund, with little expansion and still high unemployment. A seaman ashore in his home city sometimes feels isolated from the everyday life of his family and friends, longs for the weekends when there will be company in the pub, and indeed can find the whole experience an anticlimax giving way to depression. I still was in such a depression when I received a phone call from Oslo, Norway two days before Christmas.

In those days a phone call from England was an event denoting a degree of urgency meriting much discussion but a phone call from abroad was an eight-day wonder. A Norwegian shipowner called Christian-Smith had a cargo vessel in Antwerp and there was no Radio Officer available in Norway. Now one thing that I had learned from the Greeks was how to bargain. I asked the Norwegian for a salary of £100 per month which was more than a British captain earned at the time and to my surprise he agreed to pay it for one trip. The next morning I was on my way to Antwerp by air, which in itself was no small wonder at that time. A chauffeur-driven limousine met me at the airport and whisked me off to the port where I was taken on board a fine newly built vessel of about eleven thousand tons. The ship was named the Beljeanne and she was a remarkable vessel with huge jumbo derricks at every hatch.

BELFAST CITY IN THE 1950s

AMONG THE VIKINGS

The jumbo derricks were to lift the heaviest cargoes available, which at that time were railway locomotives, and the ship was stabilised by flooding special ballast tanks at the opposite side. This was the invention of Captain Christian-Smith, who went on to be a successful ship owner. There is a model of the Beljeanne today in the maritime museum in Oslo. I was no sooner on board when the sailors threw off the ropes and we moved down the river Shelte and into the North Sea. The radio room contained equipment I had never seen before, and not only was it made in Belgium but it was labelled in Norwegian. Fortunately there were some operating manuals which were written in English and I managed to get a traffic report away to Radio Antwerp. As the ship was Norwegian I called up Radio Oslo to see if there were any messages for us and, after some initial misunderstanding due to my inability to communicate in Norwegian, the operator told me he had no less than thirty telegrams for me. When the texts are in English there is an ability to forecast the rest of the letters in a word after the first couple of letters, which means that mental concentration is not strained. However, when all the words are in a foreign language there is no knowing what is coming next and total concentration is required. After an hour's intensive concentration I had all the telegrams copied but alas the texts were meaningless as they only contained numbers. I indicated my bafflement to the shore operator and he just told me to ask the skipper. This I did and the old man told me that I would find a code book in the drawer with a list of Norwegian greetings and so it was: number 1 was 'Merry Christmas and a Happy New Year', number two was 'Seasons greetings to my son', etc. etc.

This was my induction into the Norwegian Merchant Navy, one of hectic commercial working as telegrams passed to and fro to Oslo. The Captain wanted then to speak, via H/F radio-telephone, to his mother who lived on top of a mountain in Norway. To my surprise he was able to tell me how to operate the R.T. as he had been a radio operator himself before sitting his mate's ticket. There is a very sensible practice that a R.O.'s time at sea counts as sea time for the deck department and as deck apprentices spend most of their time painting and chipping, it seems that sea legs are the only benefit of sea time that they get. Anyway I contacted the coast station by W.T. (morse) and he told me to listen out on a certain freqency. Search the dial as I did, I could not pick up his signal on the R.T. frequency, and eventually the Captian told me to abandon the attempt.

I retired to my cabin and threw myself on the bunk to sleep an exhausted sleep as the ship pitched and rolled its way down the English Channel. Next morning being Christmas day, I had a chance to meet my fellow officers at a fairly formal Chrismas lunch and was delighted to find that they all spoke good English, and that everything was as clean as a whistle. We had the choice of milk, tea and coffee with every meal which started off with cold plum soup that was refreshing and not too sweet. Everybody seemed to be fair haired and over six feet tall which suited me fine as I am over six foot myself. The stewardess was the cook's wife which, again, seemed a sensible arrangement and there were other women on board which seemed to have a civilising effect. I found myself washing and dressing for meal times which became a social occasion with all conversation switching to English as soon as I appeared. This I found to be typical of the natural courtesy and consideration offered to me by my Norwegian shipmates. I found that I could follow the gist of the conversation anyway, as the Norwegian language has many words which are the same as German.

The Norwegians set a standard of cleanliness which I had missed on the Greek ship, everything being newly painted and the cabins thoroughly cleaned every day. Now it is sloppy thinking to generalise and stereotype, but it must be said that if high standards are set in a society, people will strive to attain them both on land and at sea.

The officers' steward was an intelligent lad from the Basque land in Spain who had taught himself English after escaping from Franco's Spain by trekking over the Pyrenees by night. He told me that the Basque language was purely folklore, that Basque nationalism was supported only by a minority of fanatics and that the three-headed monster of the church, the army and the industrialists kept the fascists in power. I could see a similarity in Eire, though the monster there had only two heads as there was a paucity of industrialists. The Captain was a rough diamond who had done my job and appreciated my efforts to send and copy in the Norwegian language. He had his wife and small child on board, both of whom spent a lot of time following him around to make sure he wasn't drinking. Unobserved, he would come into the radio room with a glass of whiskey which he would leave behind the door and later on he would return to drink it.

Apparently he had similar hiding places all over the ship.

On Christmas night there was a party in the Captain's cabin where all the officers sat round the table for a sumptuous meal with wine, beer and aquavit. The Captain's four year old son kept banging the table with his spoon, shouting a word which apparently is unspeakable in Norwegian. I ventured the opinion to the mate that the child had learnt it from the sailors but the mate assured me that he had learnt it from his father. All in all, I remember with fond feelings this Christmas dinner with the convivial company of people whose lives are shaped by the sea and who make the best of it. Later that evening the officers were invited to the sailors' mess where an improvised stage had been erected and the seamen mounted a cabaret with humourous sketches based on incidents during the voyage. One of the sailors had written the sketches and by the laughter they aroused it was apparent that they had hit their mark.

I had never been to Norway and was surprised to learn that it had only a population of 4 million, but with that of Sweden, it had the highest standard of living in the world. The Norwegian Merchant Navy was the second biggest in the world after Britain, and this industry accounted for much of its wealth, in a country that is mostly mountainous, and has very little in the way of natural resources. Norway also had a very comprehensive welfare system which of course is paid for by those who have plenty, which included myself, as I was on very high wages and had to pay my share of tax.

Gale force winds marked our progress across the North Atlantic, but very little outside of normal ship's routine occurred except a telegram to tell us our loading port was Norfolk, Virginia, where we would take on coal for West Germany. Then, on New Year's Day, within medium wave distance of the American coast, an S.O.S. call came over the air waves loud and clear 'S.O.S. S.O.S. Norwegian ship Haugesund. Engine room explosion. Sinking fast.' A deadly silence fell over the once morse chattering ether, and a ship that attempted a commercial call was soon silenced abruptly by the American shore station. The casualty's position was given and I rushed to the bridge with the message. The Captain, who had been drinking, doused his head in cold water and rushed to the bridge. An estimated position was calculated based on the steaming time from the noon position, and it was reckoned that we were thirty miles off the casualty. We were steaming at half speed due to the gale force conditions and the engineers put the engine on full revs. There was an air of anxiety as the Norwegians felt for their fellow countrymen in peril in the cold Altantic waves.

I called the coast station giving our position and stating our course, going full steam ahead to the stricken vessel. Another Norwegian vessel was also near at hand and it too was racing towards the casualty. Then that leviathan of the sea, the Queen Mary, called up to say that she was fifty miles off and was racing at thirty knots to the vessel. This meant that the 'Mary' would be at the scene in under two hours, but would that be soon enough for a ship that was sinking fast? We could only hope that the lifeboats had got away. The time went by without further calls from the stricken ship and when I got an up-to-date position from the bridge, I called the coast station with it and asked for an up-to-date position from the casualty. To my astonishment, the Haugesund called back to ask what the problem was, as there was no emergency on his ship and why was everybody racing towards him? The American coast station called him to say that an S.O.S. had been sent from his vessel and it was co-ordinating the rescue. The coast station asked all those involved to send their radio logs to the American coastguard as, no doubt, there would be an inquiry. Everybody was relieved that there was no danger to life on the Haugesund, but were very angry at the hoax. The consensus on board was that while the radio officer was off watch, someone on the Haugesund, who had radio training, sent the S.O.S. either as a prank or because of some grievance. Some minutes later, the Queen Mary hove into sight through the Atlantic mists like a skyscraper of the sea, towering hundreds of feet above us and ploughing through the mountainous seas at thirty knots, without a sign of a dip or roll. Truly an awesome sight, never to be seen again, as she now lies permanently moored to a wharf in California as a monument to the bygone age of transport.

Hampton Roads is the sea area outside Norfolk, Virginia, where the merchant ships wait their turn to load. Several dozen merchant men of all flags were lying at anchor, all 'light' ship and all waiting to load coal for Europe. American coal was cheap at the time, but it seemed ridiculous to me that Polish coal was being sent to South America when it was needed in Germany, which could be reached by train in a day. However, such is the logic of the market place which still seems to hold sway today.

A relaxed atmosphere pervaded the ship once anchor was dropped. Beer was served with meals and it became obvious that the six foot three mate was drunk, as well as several members of the crew. After the abstemiousness of the Greeks, it came as rather a shock to me, but then I remembered that these men lived in a cold climate with long winters to face, and it is a poor heart that never rejoices.

Norfolk, being the headquarters of the US Atlantic Fleet, was crowded with uniformed US sailors, bars were called taverns, and the barmaids would ask you for identification if they thought you were under twenty-one. Black people were confined to their own bars, seats in the bus station were labelled 'white' or 'coloured', and I wondered if the coloured section had as many sailor traps as the white section had. I paused to glance in a jeweller's shop window in the long main street. The blond assistant winked at me so I hurried in to make her aquaintance. Immediately I set foot in the shop, the owner advanced on me asking what item of jewellery I required. I saw the trap too late, but managed to redeem myself by asking for a watch strap, which was the cheapest item in the shop.

Later on that night I joined a party of our sailors in a taxi trip to a night club outside town. They were all young men in their early twenties who had been on the night watch and hadn't had any sleep and, although they all spoke English, they were tired and lapsed into Norwegian when speaking to one another. Immediately a waitress was over to our table telling them in authoritive tones to speak English and to sit up straight. It was all too much. We decided to give the night life of Norfolk a miss, go back to the ship and save our money for more welcoming hosts in Europe.

Next day we moved alongside the pier at the oddly named Newport News, which is a small town at the other side of the river from Norfolk. As the coal granules came cascading down the shoots into our holds, I walked along the pier to find my old ship the Micap also loading. I was overcome with a strange feeling of sadness and also remoteness. This ship had brought me to Poland where I had met my intended, it had been my home for four months, the scene of trials and anxiety, and there it was as if nothing had ever happened in it, just a lump of floating iron.

Soon we were on our way again across the stormy wintery Atlantic, the coal dust swept from the ship by the first roller breaking on the deck. The chattering morse is thick in these sea lanes, but I managed to pick out the familiar call sign of my old ship the Okeanis. I sent greetings to all on board and learned that she was bound for Cuba with a general cargo from Hull. Cuba at that time was a hothouse of gambling, prostitution and corruption, under a cruel military dictator favoured and protected by the US State Department. I wished to be on board the Okeanis as I knew that there was an insurrection in the mountains and that Batista's Cuba would not last. To see the last of a dying Dictatorship is a great comfort to a travelling man.

We sailed up the crowded English Channel with hundreds of British ships calling the coast stations with their traffic reports, the ones heading to home ports full of seamen with that peculiar homecoming excitement known as the 'channels'. For the Norwegians, however, there was no 'channels', as mostly they never saw their homeland except when they left their ships on leave. Some of the crew had not been home for seven years.

The river pilot for the Weser was on board, the fast broad river giving us our first even keel for eleven days. Our discharging port was the small town of Nordenham across the river from Bremerhaven, in the flat platteland of Germany. It was a pleasant seaport town spared the war damage that engulfed the bigger ports. The Basque steward and myself found our way to a bar full of our sailors who were roistering with some bar girls, who seemed to be fluent in Norwegian as well as English and Greek. No doubt there is some truth in the rumour that the British Foreign Office advises its young diplomats to sleep with the local women in order to learn the language. Fortunately, by this time I was fluent enough in German to ask about a 'local' where we could meet more salubrious company, and we were directed to a large and pleasant bar where there was a small dance band. The seats were arranged around the edge of the dance floor so I ventured across to ask a pretty girl, who was sitting on her own, to dance. I found that she could understand my German and as she pressed her body close to mine, I could be forgiven for thinking that my intentions were not unwelcome. The band stopped playing and the girl still held my hand and led me back to her table where she was joined by another girl. I was aware at the time that we were being observed by the other clientele, which is usual in any small town in any part of the world. I muttered something about having 'eine Freund mit' and walked across the floor to fetch my Spanish friend. The Spaniard, who, like most of his countrymen, valued his dignity above all else, agreed to join us at the girls' table to make a foursome, so we both traversed the floor in full view of everyone. To my embarrassment and to the Spaniard's horror, the two German girls were now seated with their obviously long-standing boyfriends who looked at us like a 'pig pissing', as they say in County Antrim. So again we had to traverse the floor in full view of everyone, with the Spaniard spitting curses in his own language and calling me a 'son-of-a-bitch' for making him look ridiculous. Luckily I could see the humour in the situation and had a good laugh, knowing that the girl had obviously contrived the situation to make her boyfriend jealous. In the end we both did manage to escort young women home and I have memories of an angry mother calling from the upstairs window of a shop to her daughter about the lateness of the hour, and the equal anger of the father, using much the same language as parents everywhere.

The next morning a tall, young Norwegian arrived on the quayside, fresh from radio school in Oslo, ready to take over my job in the radio room. I had hoped that the ship owner would have forgotten about my high rate of pay and let me stay on, but obviously Captain Christian-Smith did not become rich by forgetting such things and I had to go. It was then that I realised something about myself. I was no longer looking forward to going home and had become what the Greeks call a 'Sea Gipsy'.

The Norwegian law insists that all seafarers must sign off ship's articles in the nearest Norwegian Consulate, probably as a safeguard against abandonment by unscrupulous ship owners, so I bade my farewells and caught the train to Bremen. The Consul there told me to book a flight to Belfast and charge all my expenses to him, which seemed very generous, as on British ships, once you have signed off you are also off the payroll. Anyway, the hotel and the travel agent seemed to know the procedure and accepted my signature without question, as did the taxi driver and night cashier of the club where I spent most of the night.

A German night club has an atmosphere of decadence and frenetic activity very like the musical 'Cabaret', based on Auden and Isherwood's book on pre-Hitler Berlin. A compelling place for rootless, lost souls, where music and company can be bought for money. Fascinated by the string of conjurers, comedians and jazz singers, I sat there alone for two hours, watching the two other tables that were occupied by escapists such as myself. The snow was falling gently over the newly restored mediaeval city of Bremen as I sped along in a taxi for the airport the next day. Back in Belfast, the winter rain shrouded the Cavehill and a wreath of damp fog surrounded my mind. My true home was a clean, well found ship amongst the Vikings.

DOWN AND OUT IN LONDON

I waited for two weeks for a call from the Union to join another ship, but in vain. Eventually, like many another, I took the boat to England and the train down to London. I settled into the Red Ensign Club which was an excellent establishment, run for the benefit of merchant seamen who, like myself, were waiting on a berth. It was run by the Merchant Navy establishment, composed of representatives of the unions, the ship owners and the government, and conveniently situated at Aldgate East, close to the docks and also near enough to the shipping company offices in the city. There was also a Merchant Navy hotel, solely for officers, at Lancaster Gate, but it was expensive and away from the shipping milieu in the East End.

The majority of the clientele of the Red Ensign were seamen who had just signed off a ship and were too late for a rail connection home, but there were also sea gipsies who had no homes other than ships. Among these were a group of Poles, who had been in the Polish Army in the West, and decided to opt for the Merchant Navy on demobilization. They would sit quietly talking Polish in a corner or watch television programmes that they could barely understand. For an immigrant, the sea is a bad choice for a career, as there is nowhere to put down roots, and I hoped that these lonely men were saving their wages in anticipation of setting up home in Britain. Then there were the alcoholics who would be in the bar from opening time, steadily drinking all day, until their leave was up, and becoming noisy and incoherent as night drew nigh. For them, the benefit of sea life was that they would be forced to give their livers a rest when they went back to sea. The other group of semi-permanent residents were the men who had more than three 'D.R's' on their discharge books. 'D.R.' meant 'declined to report', indicating bad conduct. With three D.R.'s, a seaman was reckoned to be unemployable, but there was always a chance that the Shipping Federation, or 'pool', would be short handed and that they would get a berth.

While on the Okeanis, I had learnt the names of the principal Greek ship owners such as Kulakundia, Embericos, Niarchos, Goulandris and Hadjipateras, who all had offices in London, so I visited them all in person with my ticket in my hand. I was always respectfully received and my name and address noted, as a radio officer could fall sick or leave at any time and a ship could not sail without one.

I visited a friend who was living in London, a former cook on the Queen Mary, who had married an American girl and who was preparing to emigrate there, now that he was over twenty six and no longer liable for military service in the U.S. As travel was costly and lengthy in those days, emigrants to America expected not to see their friends and relatives again for decades, so it was a sad parting. However, as it turned out, we had an earlier reunion than expected.

Goulandris Shipping called the Red Ensign one Friday morning and offered me a job, so I hurried over to their offices in the oddly named St. Mary Axe to make arrangements. As they owned both the Micape and the Okeanis, they knew I could do the job and they urgently required a man to fly to the Portuguese island of Maderia. They also had a job coming up in Philadelphia the next week, so I could have had my choice. At that time Maderia had no airport so they proposed to charter a flying boat in Southampton to fly me out, and presumably land on the sea off Fuchal. However, when I heard that the reason there was a vacancy was that the radio officer had hanged himself in his cabin, I decided to wait and take the job in Philadelphia. Apparently the poor guy had received a letter from his wife stating that she had divorced him, and he could not handle the grief.

Saddened by the suicide of a fellow radio officer, I returned to the club at three thirty in the afternoon, to find to my dismay that the banks were now closed for the weekend and that I had only ten shillings to see me through until Monday. My friend Hugh had already left for Southampton, I didn't know another soul in London, so what was I to do? Luckily I had paid for my room in advance so I would not be evicted. I bought my tea in the dining room and I had enough left for breakfast in the morning, but from there on it seemed I would have to starve. I had several hundred pounds in my bank account but no means of getting at it. After breakfast on the Saturday I sat in the lounge with the Poles, the sea gipsies, the 'DR' men and, as if by intuition, a Scots steward got into conversation with me over the subject of getting a few bob for a meal. How he knew that I was broke I don't know, but know he did, and set about re-assuring me about getting food without payment. 'Wait until the bar opens and the "pay-offs" buy their sausage rolls and sandwiches', he said. 'Sometimes they leave an end or even a whole one, and if you can spot it before the barman does, its yours'.

Sure enough, when the bar opened, men with suitcases came round after paying off at the 'pool' and ordered pints of beer and sandwiches. Being flush with money they would order more than they consumed and before the barman could clear the counter my Scots friend had the uneaten sandwich over to our table. 'It's yours, Sparkie', he said. 'You are new to this game.' In such a way we managed to keep our bellys full over the weekend. The Scot had been a chief steward who had been caught in some fiddle and was on the run from the courts over maintainance to his wife. When he heard that I had to join a ship the next week and had money in the bank he never left my side. He even managed to borrow money on the strength of the fact that he was friendly with 'Sparks' who was waiting for the banks to open on Monday morning.

Monday came and the loyal Scot accompanied me everywhere and of course I paid for his meals and drinks and finally he accompanied me to the airport where he chided me about my ex-Royal Navy canvas suitcase, saying 'It isn't fit for a transatlantic traveller and an officer.' He put the bite on me for a fiver, which in those days was a week's wages, but although I knew I was being imposed upon, I gave it to him and wished him good luck.

The Pan Am plane I boarded was cramped and noisy and seemed hardly in the air when it touched down again at Shannon Airport where big West of Ireland men in voluminous brown overcoats escorted us to Nissen huts where there were two dormitories, one for male passengers and the other for females. After five hours sleep we were again herded on board the plane where breakfast was served by surly stewards who then promptly turned in on the special sleeping berths that they had. A ten hour journey, broken by a short stop in frozen Prince Edward Island, took us into La Guardia Airport in New York and, all in all, it was the most uncomfortable, unglamourous experience of travel that I have ever had.

By this time it was ten at night in New York, no-one was there to meet me and I had no idea of where to go. Fortunately I had an American dollar in my wallet and phoned the shipping company which, to my great relief, had an answering service. The girl on duty told me to take a taxi to a Greek hotel on Forty-Second Street and to get the desk clerk to pay the taxi. I was surprised that the taximan would take a fare on such an uncertain method of payment, but he did, and sure enough the desk clerk, on hearing that I was from Orion Shipping, paid the taximan and showed me to my room. It was surely the scruffiest hotel in either Greece or America, the carpet being threadbare and greasy, the wallpaper brown and stained, and the rags of curtains unable to hold out the blinking neon lights from Time Square which was just round the corner.

My first glimpse of New York by daylight was on the morning of St. Patrick's Day and the majesty of the huge man-made canyons was awesome to behold. The styles of dress, the size and shapes of the cars, the roar of traffic were so different from anything experienced in Europe that I stood on Broadway culture-shocked beyond belief. The old Irish snake charmer was being honoured in the New World later on and crowds were already gathered in Broadway, decked out in green hats and ribbons. Many swarthy Mediterranean faces sported green rosettes and one obviously Puerto Rican girl sported a metal badge proclaiming 'St. Joe's' in the fly of her jeans. I drifted with the crowd to the crash barrier where one of New York's finest snarled and glared at the crowds like a bad tempered lunatic asylum attendant, swinging his night stick as if to say 'Make my day by stepping past the barrier'. The bands paraded twelve across, bearing names like 'Notre Dame', 'St. Bernadettes', and 'Cross and Passion', swaggering politicians with green sashes waved to the crowds, and it was easy to see from a cursory glance that every race on the planet was represented and what was happening was a manifestation of Catholic power in New York City. At the end of the parade came the Irish county associations with banners resplendent with round towers, bearded patriarchs and departing snakes. After them came the 'Freedom Fighters' with their sinister messages of hate: 'England get out of Ireland', 'Boycott British goods', etc. I don't think any of this had any impact on the crowd, most of whom would have had only a very hazy idea of where Ireland actually was. No doubt it made the marchers feel good to forget the failure of independant Ireland to give them a living at home and blame it all on England.

The next day my ship had docked at Philadelphia, so I made my way to the splendid Grand Central Station to board a train for the city of 'brotherly love'. An American train ride was then something of an experience: the seats were as on a bus, with black guys bringing trays of hot dogs and delicious piping hot coffee every half hour or so. There was a glass-sided observation carriage at the back where you could smoke and where it was generally agreed you could strike up conversations with complete strangers.

The ship turned out to be a T2 tanker, mass-produced by Henry Kaiser during the war, but excellent ships none the less. Everything on board was made of light metal including the furniture and the accommodation included a spacious cabin, shower and toilet all ensuite. The vessel had been converted to bulk cargo from liquid by opening the decks and adding steel hatch covers, and leaving the side oil storage tanks for carrying oil cargoes as well. To do this the ship had been in a Japanese shipyard where they also lengthened the ship by cutting it in half and inserting a hull piece of fifty feet. It took the shipyard three months to make these changes and during this time the crew remained on board and had a free holiday in Japan. It is interesting to note that Goulandris Bros decided to do this with all their T2 tankers and the other ones took only six weeks to alter. This meant the T2s were avaible for either oil or ore cargoes, which ever was the most profitable.

I was replacing a young Canadian R.O who had spent a year on the vessel which was named the Andros Saturn. The environs of the ship were the usual chaos of a ship replacing crew and taking on stores, but I managed to be of use on the first day aboard. The electrician was an Italian whose passport expired while at sea, so the U.S. Immigration put him under armed guard and this man followed him everywhere he went, even to the toilet. Luckily the guard, whose huge revolver was strapped to his side, was an Italian-American so they could converse in Italian, but I offered to take the out-of-date passport to the Italian consul in New York for renewal. This seemed satisfactory to all sides so I caught the next train to New York, found the Italian consul, had the passport stamped and had a meal in one of the excellent Schraft's coffee shops, when I happened to glance at the incoming liners column in the New York Times. The Mauretania was due in New York that very evening, carrying my good friend Hugh and his wife from London, so by unbelievable coincidence I had arrived in the States before them.

I finished my coffee and, in high excitement, rushed to pier forty-two where the Mauretania was just being tied up. There were hundreds of people there, porters rushing about, immigration men shouting for Polish speakers, policemen forcing people behind the barriers again, and general confusion. Hugh was going to stay with his in-laws in Chicago and presumably they would help him find his feet in his new country and probably they would keep him and their daughter for some time. I saw

Hugh's blond head, a good foot above the rest of the crowd pushing a luggage cart with his heavily pregnant wife and little dogs bringing up the rear. I could only croak 'Hugh, Joan, its Derek' as I had lost my voice due to the sudden change of climate in America. They were amazed to see me and so were Joan's parents who appeared in a moment. They had travelled from Chicago to help with the luggage and they must have thought that I had arrived with Hugh and was some relation, possibly a brother, as we were both fair-haired and over six feet tall. Anyway, we repaired to a hotel near the pier and, while the daughter and parents were sorting out accommodation, my friend and I went round the corner for a drink. The bar man caught our accents immediately (he was from North Belfast), so the three of us were drawn into a mist of old Belfast nostalgia much to the annoyance of the other customers who were shamefully neglected.

Returning to the hotel we sat down to eat a meal which was memorable for many reasons. As I had a bad laryngitis due to the change in temperatures between London and New York, I was not able to contribute much to the conversation. I could see that Hugh's father-in-law was plainly puzzled as to who I was, as I had apparently arrived with his son-in-law. The father-in-law was plainly worried that he was going to have to keep me as well as his daughter's husband. He asked me where I was going, and my croaked answer of 'Peru' was plainly ridiculous. Eventually Hugh explained to him how we made our farewells a week previously in London and by amazing coincidence I was in New York before them and was able to greet them at the pier. I noticed the lines around the old man's mouth lighten as it sunk in that I was not going to charge in on him in Chicago.

My friend Hugh later went on to be a successful businessman in Chicago but I was not to see him again for twenty years, by which time he had three beautiful teenage daughters. He survived a heart attack and alcoholism and like many other immigrants was thinking of ending his days in his native city when he succumbed to lung cancer. He attributed this to being on board the big liners when they were refitting, when everything was ripped out, including asbestos linings, and the air would be thick with dust.

The Andros Saturn eased out of Philadelphia down the Delaware River to a small town on the river bank called Marcus Hook where the giant Westinghouse factory was situated. Our electric diesel engines had been made there, so the chief engineer was taking advantage of its proximity to iron out some problems with the experts. Like most American company towns there was only the minimum of the amenities of civilised living, such as the drug store. It was owned by a Greek who was glad to see some of his compatriots and who told me that 90% of the bored youths in his establishment were Irish, meaning of couse that they were of Irish descent. I thought of the high hopes of their ancestors setting out for the new world only to end up in a place like Marcus Hook where all there was was work.

The Captain of the Andros Saturn was a very erudite university-educated man who had a deal of knowledge about world politics and indeed of English and Anglo-Irish literature, and both he and his wife became good friends of mine. He was able to explain to me about the power and corruption of the Greek shipowners who apparently controlled the Greek establishment from their offices in London and New York. One of the shipowners wanted to be able to call himself captain but had not the neccessary sea time or ticket, so the parliament passed a law that a person with so much sea time and so much service in the Greek Navy was entitled to call himself captain. Only the shipowner had this sea time and the same amount of service in the navy, so he was the only beneficiary of this law.

The third mate, who was uncertificated, was a huge Cretan and had just been at sea for one year, at the age of twenty-nine. This was because his father had been in the resistance during the German occupation and had also been the mayor of his town. Because of this, the right wing government had conscripted the son into the army and kept him there for five years as a possible subversive. Then when he was released from military service he couldn't get a passport to start his career in navigation. All this happened in a country that was part of NATO guarding us from totalitarianism.

SOUTH TO PERU

Soon we were into the pleasant Caribbean weather, with flying fish landing on the deck, while the Captain and myself debated the rights of man and the evils of neo colonial exploitation in what we were about, carrying away the natural resources of a third world country for the benefit of Bethlehem Steel. Again through the wondrous Miraflores locks in the Panama Canal into the Pacific and down the west coast of Colombia, Equador and Peru. We berthed at a small mining village called San Juan, which boasted only a long jetty linked by rail with the iron ore mine. The iron ore was loaded from the rail wagons by mechanical grabs, causing clouds of iron ore dust everywhere. The portholes had to be bolted tight in the stifling heat otherwise your bedding and clothes would be coated in fine yellow dust. The village was purely a mining settlement, the prefabricated houses for the workers lined up like huts in an army camp. The population was entirely Peruvian Indian, squat little brown people who seemed to have no necks, mostly around five foot tall. Indeed it was easy to see that they were of Asiatic origin, having, as they did, the same mongolian features as the Japanese and Chinese.

    I never managed to get into the iron ore mine to see the conditions but I must say the housing seemed reasonable compared with what I had seen elsewhere in the third world. There was a market taking place just beside the pier with heaps of vegetables, sweet meats, coca cola and the like. I purchased a bag of boiled sweets to give to the children and was soon besieged by urchins pulling and tugging at my clothes. In order to extricate myself I scattered the wrapped sweets on the ground, hoping they would detach themselves from me, when to my horror the adults scrambled in the dust as well as the children. I felt ashamed at inflicting such indignity on any people, but it showed the depth of their deprivation that they would submit themselves to it. As I write, the Shining Path terrorists are exploding in a fury of revolt that is only understandable when we know to what depths these poor Indians have been drawn.

    There was a cantina of sorts on the hill above the town, which was owned by Russian immigrants. It was really a wooden shack in the desert that sold bottled beer and some undrinkable spirits, with some Greek taverna music in the juke box, which led me to believe that the Indians must have found the prices too high. What curious eddy in the tide of war had flung these Russians up on the edge of the Peruvian desert could only be guessed at. Our cargo was destined for Philadelphia again, much to the disgust of the crew who found the Americans hostile to non-English speakers and the prices dearer than Europe.

It is a curious phenomenom of life that in countries made up of immigrants there is latent hostility to new arrivals. The steward was a young, excitable man with a good flow of broken English who went out of his way to talk to me, I suspect to impress his colleagues. One day the officers got very upset about the quality of the meal and with typical Greek volubility and arm waving they upbraided him, although as far as I was concerned the meal was much the same as any other. The steward summoned the aged cook from the galley and they defended his creations with much vigour. It never ceased to amaze me how much verbal abuse the Greeks could take without resorting to fisticuffs, as such shouting would inevitably lead to blows on a British ship. Later on that evening there was a commotion in the area of the saloon which I investigated, only to find the steward drunk, crying, and beating his head off the bulkhead. The scene would have caused ribald derision on a British ship but in this case the very ones who had been castigating the steward were now consoling him, and eventually carried him to his cabin where they put him to bed, soothing and clucking over him as one would a frightened child.

We passed through the Panama Canal again and there in the other side of the Miraflores locks was the gleaming white shape of the Beljeanne, the Norwegian cross fluttering at her stern. This is a rare moment at sea, when the opportunity arises to see again your former shipmates. I shouted over to the sailors on the deck, waving the while, calling 'Nisten', which is the Norse equivalent of the nickname 'Sparks'. The Spanish cabin steward with whom I was friendly, appeared on deck and gave the clenched fist communist salute right under the noses of the American Marine guards on the shore. They probably thought he was just angry about something.

The rest of the voyage up the east coast of North America was uneventful except for a stinging toothache which I developed when we entered the Delaware River. This is what every sailor dreads the most, a toothache that cannot be assuaged without recourse to a dentist. The pain was maddening, and it took a further twenty-four hours before we tied up at Philadelphia. The Captain had arranged with the ship's agent to rush me to a dentist and, lo and behold, when the dentist inspected my mouth the pain vanished and he could find no unsound teeth.

The berth we had seemed to be on the outskirts of the city, encased in a huge compound surround by a twelve foot palisade. The compound contained the steelworks and the docks which were worked by sweating Negroes who shovelled the ore into the metal grabs when the ore became inaccessible. This work went on day and night, often spoiling our sleep, when the huge grabs would bang against the ship's side, shaking its whole structure. At these times I wondered if the impacts would spring the welds on the bulkheads but the engineers assured me they had welding equipment aboard if any leaks occurred. The gates to the compound were manned by armed company guards who apparently had power to shoot at any intruders, although why anyone would want to enter that dusty floodlit hell was beyond me.

Outside the gates lay miles of brownstone, crumbling, scabrous tenements, teeming with black families in conditions I have only seen in the Georgian tenements of Dublin in the forties. There seemed to be thousands of people on the streets, of every shade from high yellow to purple black. Sometimes they would call out to me but I found their speech unintelligible and thought it best to pretend not to understand English. There was a bus stop at the gates of a hospital where a policeman was standing. At first I thought he was waiting for a bus but he told me he had to wait there all night as there would be 'cuttings' coming in by ambulance. 'Cuttings' apparently was a black idiom for stabbings and he had to be on hand to take statements from the victims as to the identity of their attackers. The policeman, who was obviously bored and glad of a listening ear, went on to tell me that the victims seldom named their attackers, who would have been mostly relatives.

I took a bus into Penn Centre, which was a collection of skyscrapers with some landscaping and some shopping centres inbetween, which served as the heart of the city. Somehow the pristine symmetry of this contrived city centre didn't work and I have seen this so often, when an artificially contrived focal point of a conurbation is ignored by the inhabitants. Wandering down a tree-lined avenue I chanced on a neon-lighted, single-story building announcing with the aid of lurid arrows that it was a night club. With a resignation born of experience I paid a few dollars entrance with the expectation of being legally robbed as an 'out of towner', as strangers in any American city are known. To my surprise it turned out to be a pleasant area of tables where one could sit alone without trouble and listen to a full swing orchestra playing the Glenn Millar hit tunes and the like. The waitresses were polite and prompt, without being obsequious. I had by accident stumbled into a wholesome place of social intercourse for American youth, so unlike the sleazy fleshpots where seamen usually congregate. I danced with a tall girl of Polish extraction who invited me to her home where I met her parents and grandparents, who had come from what Americans call the 'old country'.

The grandparents had come from Poland early in the century and still didn't speak enough English to sustain a conversation. As I had been in Poland they were interested to find out what Poland was like under socialism, as they had heard that religion was banned and that the young people were going off to hotels every weekend to engage in Godless debauchery. The main link to the homeland for the emigrant in the U.S. is through the Church, which has masses in the various languages, said usually by ethnic priests, so the only information coming out for those who had lost touch with relatives was through the sermons on Sundays. I was able to assure them that there were very few hotels in Poland in which the young could debauch, that sexual morals seemed to me to be no different than anywhere else, and that some of the clergy supported the reconstruction and industrialisation that the Polish government was undertaking.

The girl's father worked in a steel mill, earned good money and I could see that the detached wooden house in which they lived was of a higher standard than any worker's house in Europe. The industrial working class at that time in the U.S. had achieved a high standard of living due to the militancy of the unions, whose power alas now has been broken by the mass immigration of Latin Americans and Asians. Also the McCarthy witch hunts robbed the trade unions of many of their best leaders.

This decent Polish family took me out on the Sunday to see the Valley Forge museum which was a recreation of the civil war battle on the actual site. I wrote to the girl for a while but thought it prudent to tail off the letters to prevent a hurt to her and her family.

I made contact with the Irish-Americans through the Chief Immigration Officer in Philadelphia, whose parents came from Maghera, County Londonderry. He assumed, like most Americans, that I would be Catholic and told me the times of the masses in the nearest Catholic Church.

Rather than explain to him that most Ulstermen were Protestants I thanked him and let it go. The next time he came on board he told me that if I wanted to stay in the U.S. he could fix it for me. I had no desire to stay in America as I had a lot more of the world to see, but I thought of the poor Greeks who would give their eye teeth to be working for American wages, and would have to wait ten years for a place on the Greek immigration quota.

With our ship emptied, hosed down and replenished with stores, we set off down the Delaware River again, slipping into the ship's watch routine, with the only thing to joyfully anticipate being the bottles of beer with our meals on Wednesday and Friday. These were also meatless days in the Greek Orthodox calender, when we would eat boiled cod or fried herrings with their heads still attached. I never got used to eating the fish with it's beady eye seemingly fixed on mine, but the Greeks, unlike the Irish, regarded the fish days as a feast rather than penance. The attitude of most of them to religion was of healthy scepticism, but some of them would have very graphic ikons in their cabins, showing an all powerful Jesus figure above the storm clouds guiding a heroic helmsman through the waves which would be breaking over his vessel. Others would have ikons to Saint Dimitrious, the patron saint of seamen, which if lowered into a stormy sea, reputedly would calm the waves. One of the sailors, who trumpeted his scepticism in the sailors' mess, was observed doing just that at the dead of night.

Our aged cook, who must have been well into his seventies, cut his hand on a boning knife as we sailed down the west coast of South America on our way again to load iron ore in San Juan. The wound festered, he became toxic, and it was clear that something had to be done. The Captain, whose English was perfect, worded a radio medical to WSL New York, which I duly transmitted. I received back a telegram listing all the steps to be taken to lance the old man's wound, apply an antiseptic and bind it up with a dressing. A crowd of 'off watch' sailors and firemen had gathered round the door of the cook's cabin to watch this operation. The Captain, it must be said, was a nervous man so it was arranged that I would hold the bowl of hot water and antiseptic while the Captain would administer the incision. The steward, always a joker, pulled a white sheet over his head like a ghost, emitting a low growling noise. The old cook offered a stream of curses from his bed, to the hoots of laughter from the crew. The Captain's hands shook with nerves as he advanced the scalpel to the cook's swollen hand, but he made the incision in the right place, releasing a stream of pus. A cheer rang out from the faces crowded round the door and porthole while I swabbed round the incision. A piece of theatre surely, so, when the cook's hand was bandaged up, there was a round of applause.

The cook was soon back at work, but always had his portholes bolted down tight, and his door locked from then on. The old man had been at sea without home leave for twelve years apparently and had confided in the Captain that, if anything happened to him, there were three thousand gold pounds in his cabin which he wanted sent to his wife in Andros. Apparently the man had five daughters and had been obliged to find a dowry for each of them, each dowry being about two thousand gold pounds. The Greeks did not trust paper money as it had a habit of losing its value overnight, especially the drachma, so they bought old British guineas which at the time were worth about three pounds each. The cook, having told the Captain his secret, knew, in the nature of things, that other people would get to know, so he was keeping his cabin sealed even in the hottest weather.

The marriage dowry was at that time an important element in the lives of Greek seamen from the islands, as the island girls did not have the chance to meet men folk as they would all be away at sea. Consequently the marriages were arranged by the fathers who would also be at sea, generally by correspondance between the ships. The cook who would have married late in life, had what was judged to be a great misfortune in having five daughters for whom to find dowries, so he found himself as a seagoing bond slave for his future sons-in-law. Hopefully now that Greece is in the E.C. all these mediaeval cash nexus marriage customs are discontinued and Greek ancient mariners are allowed to have a well earned retirement before the age of seventy.

We reached the familiar landfall of San Juan to find a Norwegian ore carrier occupying the only berth at the pier, so we had to stay at anchor until the Norwegian was loaded. This was the first time that our ship stayed overnight in Peru, and it presented an opportunity to travel to the nearest town which was eighty kilometres away from the port. The agent fixed me up with a visa to travel inland and ashore I went in his launch. A taxi appeared as if by magic on the jetty, suggesting some sort of tip off on the agent's part, but, as the asking price for the round journey to Nasca was only four American dollars, I didn't quibble. It was dark when the old Buick taxi lumbered up the sandy hill and over the desert following a line of stones laid out on the sand. The driver was an Indian who kept repeating 'toda la noche' to reassure me that he would wait for me all night. Some miles out into the desert a group of Indians dressed in soft hats and blankets stood huddled together beside the road. To my surprise my driver stopped the taxi and they all piled in. They were very exotic people in their coloured blankets and what appeared to be trilby hats with feathers. They spoke an Indian language to the driver and completely ignored my presence, leading me to believe that what I was paying for was a community bus. Still no matter, the Indians were dropped off at the outskirts of Nasca which was really only a fair sized town, just like one sees in western. With peeling stucco, unpaved streets, Indians squatting against the walls, a perfect set for Viva Zapata.I noticed however that all the cafes, bars, and shops were shuttered and the driver explained that it was a Saint's Day so everything was closed. The hotel, for some inexplicable reason called the Port Hotel although eighty kilometres from the coast, was quite luxurious, with linen table-cloths, silver service and air conditioning. It was fine to have a meal with wine, away from the smell of diesel, the chatter of a language I could not understand and to pretend for one evening at least to be a rich tourist visiting an exotic part of the world.

A stroll through the town revealed that the celebration of the Saint's Day meant the letting off of rockets and fireworks and the patronising of the town brothel by most of the male population. This was the most peculiar building that I have ever seen and the only one in the town that appeared to be open for business. It was built in the form of a semi-circular arcade, where strollers could walk through and examine the girls who were behind barred gates in individual rooms. Each room had a bed on a stone floor with a covered bucket which contained water for douching. The girls were young, some quite pretty, all in their underclothes, some with religious medals pinned to their bras. When they had a customer they pulled a curtain across the bars and presumably completed the transaction.

All the while rockets were screaming across the glass roof of the brothel in a double celebration of the life of the Saint. I spoke to one girl through the bars. She was tall for an Indian, had shapely thighs, and her ample bosom spilled out over her bra. She thought, naturally enough, that I was a 'Yanqui' and I was surprised that she understood where I was from when I told her I was from Ireland. This was, she said, because she had been educated by Irish priests in Lima. She saw no contradiction in what she was doing for a living and her religion. I explained that, in Ireland, the priests thought that sex was the only sin and thundered against any manifestation of it outside of marriage. She persuaded me to continue this philosophical conversation inside the room, whereupon she drew the curtains across the bars, where we then philosophied quite vigorously to the satisfaction of all concerned, except perhaps the priests in Ireland.

A taxi called for me at the hotel at dawn the next morning and we drove out over the desert to the coast. Just outside Nasca the early morning mists were rising off the sand and the high Andes loomed in the distance, with emerging sun behind them like a scorching fireball. I could see why the sun played such an important part in the Mayan culture, as it seemed about to engulf the mountains and the desert. Outside the town I watched Indian women emerge from what were literally holes in the ground to set up little piles of nuts and vegetables on handerchiefs on the ground. This was the beginnings of the day's market on the plains of Nasca, where, a thousand years before, a sophisticated and complex culture had existed.

The Swiss writer, Von Daniken, thought that the giant roadways marked out in the desert were evidence of extra terrestrial air strips, where creatures from another planet had landed, inspected us, and then wisely decided to give us a miss. The roadways, which I must admit that I never noticed although from inspection of Von Daniken's book I must have traversed, are now thought to be some sort of outdoor arena for the Mayan sun worshiping.

On the way back we were stopped by a road block operated by a single customs/immigration man who had a little hut outside the port. He had a military visored hat and a stained khaki uniform, but when I looked at his feet I saw that they were bare. He looked at my seaman's book with the Peruvian visa, took it off me and stamped it with an elaborate official stamp which he stamped the wrong way up, so I surmised that, as well as bootless, he was also a little illiterate. With previous experience of South American officialdom, I was not about to point out his mistake.

Back aboard ship there was a cheerfulness in the atmosphere caused by the news that this time our cargo was destined for Europe, Rotterdam to be precise. Europe at that time was a good deal cheaper than the U.S. and also foreign seamen were treated with respect, if only for their purchasing power.

The voyage up the coast, through the Canal and across the Atlantic, was filled with ship's routine, with nothing to break the monotony of looking out the port at the Goulandris colours of blue, yellow and black on the funnel. In my boredom, I would learn some more German and re-read old letters from Poland and from home, although, as time went by, I became less interested in the parochial affairs of my native land.

The intractable problems of Ulster were again in the news with Catholic nationalist terrorists blowing up a bridge in County Tyrone. There was also terrorism in Cyprus causing the chief engineer to speak to the Captain about his friendship with myself which he deemed inappropriate as I was a British subject. The Captain explained that I was not in agreement with British occupation of Cyprus but, as always with a bigot, he refused to separate the person from the action. It is now my view that when two ethnic groups cannot share the same country they would be better apart. Eventually the Turks invaded Cyprus, evicted the Greeks from a third of it, and there has been peace for twenty years. The same solution seems to be near at hand in Bosnia where the population is divided three ways, and one hopes that there will eventually be peace based on separateness. I would like to think that in Northern Ireland, with 40% of the minority community wishing to remain British, this drastic solution would not be necessary.

We entered the river Maas at the Hook of Holland to the waves of the sunbathers on the large beach which runs from the river estuary up the shore of the North Sea. Twenty miles or so up the river we came to what is the world's second largest harbour. Hundreds of ships of all nationalities rode at anchor in a man-made lake. Some, like our own ship, were laden to the plimsoll line with iron ore, some were huge quarter-mile-long super tankers, while others were little coastal scoots with women and children to be seen on the fantail while washing fluttered on clothes lines. Long narrow Rhine barges ploughed up and down with the flags of every European country at their stern. We had only dropped the anchor when one of them motored alongside, flung out fenders and opened its hatches. The skipper made his barge fast to our side and shouted up for loading to commence. Minutes later a launch full of Dutch dockers arrived to roll back our hatch covers and, like clockwork, a floating crane was manoeuvered alongside for unloading to commence. With efficiency like this it is no wonder that Rotterdam is Europe's busiest port.

All the crew, armed with large bundles of Dutch guilders, appeared on deck, washed and perfumed in their best shore going togs. Many of them had not been ashore for three months, finding the U.S. too expensive and unfriendly and now they were ready to dive into the fleshpots of Rotterdam where there was always a welcome for a sailor with money to spend. The harbour authorities operated a launch service which ferried the seamen to and from the shore, but first we had to go round all the ships in the harbour, picking up shore going crew from each. At any given time there would be ninety ships loading, unloading or undergoing repair at Rotterdam, so it took quite a while getting round the ones at anchor in the pool. One ship at which we stopped flew the flag of South Africa, a crowd of coloured seamen swarmed aboard the launch chattering away in an excited manner. From what I observed they were Cape coloureds, ie. a racial mixture of Indonesian, Negro and Dutch. I saw the launch skipper do a double take when he heard them speak; I could see that he was surprised to be able to understand them and obviously he knew they were not speaking Dutch. Eventually he spoke to one of them in Dutch and of course the man answered in Afrikaans which is based on the language of the Dutch settlers four hundred years ago. Some of the seamen got off at the island of Kattendracht so I went along with them to see the sights. It turned out to be a street of bars and brothels deserted in the afternoon but would obviously come alive when the daywork sailors would get shore leave.

I met a grizzled alcoholic who had been panhandling in the Red Ensign club during my sojourn in London and was glad to speak English to someone that I knew. He had been lucky enough to get a job on a coaster trading to the continent and had managed to behave himself for the two months since I had seen him. I hopped on the next launch which landed me at the city centre and followed the crowd again, this time to a huge building run by the missions to seamen. There was a souvenir shop there, and the saleswoman was surrounded by a dozen seamen of all colours and nationalities. I watched and listened to her fascinated as she answered every customer in the language of his choice. In the space of five minutes I heard her speak Greek, English, Norwegian, Spanish, Finnish, French and Portuguese, all spoken fluently and without effort. Later I found that most Dutch people were trilingual, speaking French, German and English without effort. Being at the crossroads of Europe helps, but then again the Belgians are also at this point in geography and are mostly monolingual.

I found a city bar where the barmaid was personable, where I could speak English without searching for words that I knew would be understood and managed to spend a 'king's ransom' buying drinks and buying coloured water for the barmaid. There were three nightclubs all in a row near the city centre. Each one looked like a cinema from the outside, big, rotund, and purpose-built to rob merchant seamen and visiting firemen of their money. The upmarket one cost a day's wages for a seaman just to step inside, boasted a cabaret after midnight and was frequented mostly by officers and middle aged businessmen from abroad. There were expensively dressed and coiffured women standing about like Queens of Sheba who would look at you disdainfully if you ventured to speak to them. If you asked them to dance they would as like as not refuse, yet they were all without escorts. Yet an American engineer I talked to assured me they were all whores, in the full commercial sense of the word.

An elegant, blond lady, with fine chiselled features, was perched on a bar stool beside us. She was dressed in a well-tailored suit which emphasised her shapely bottom, and I would have guessed her age to be around twenty-five and her occupation to be a boutique owner or something similar. She languidly smoked a cigarette, all the while looking at herself in the mirror with her ice blue eyes, studiously ignoring the American and myself. As if to prove a point, the American asked her to dance but she refused distainfully in flawless English. Bluntly, and I thought courageously, he then asked how much she wanted to sleep with him. With a withering look, she told him coldly that if she liked him, which she didn't, she would charge him £25, which then represented a month's wages for a Dutch docker. I thought that no wonder she dressed so well and looked so elegant; she really was more of a courtesan than a prostitute. I realised that she was not meat for my teeth but I bought her an outrageously expensive drink to discover more about her lifestyle.

She told me she would not stay long at the night club as she was going to Paris in the morning with the Brazilian Consul. He was attending a diplomatic conference there and, I gather, he would pass her off as his mistress. Now, when I glance at glossy fashion and gossip magazines, generally in waiting rooms, I look at the photographs of the rich and famous, and wonder if their elegant consorts are expensive whores like the lady in the bar. I left the night club, a week's wages the poorer, and reflected on the folly of 'cherchez la femme'.

At the landing stage I met half a dozen Greeks from other ships and engaged in a sort of parochial conversation of the sea. They wanted to know who my captain was, who was the chief steward, was there anybody there from Chios or Paxos? I realised then that these men who spent most of their life at sea had their only chance of meeting their friends and neighbours at places like Rotterdam, one of the great crossroads of the world's shipping lanes. While I had no urge to go home, I realised that I did not want to become like that, with only seagoing friends left that I might see now and again in Rotterdam or Singapore.

Next day on board, the ship was alive with tales of the adventures of the night before, of prodigious sexual deeds and money spent. The Captain had dined with his wife and the ship's chandler, also Greek, and had met some Greek officers off a Polish liner. These were men who had fought on the Communist side in the civil war and who would be imprisoned if they went back to Greece. They now lived in Gdynia with their families as political refugees, but found that their navigational and engineering skills were appreciated in the expanding Polish Merchant Navy. The ship's chandler apparently was not happy to be seen talking with them in case they were being watched by the Dutch political police who would inform the Greek Consul. Later on, when I travelled to Poland via the Hook of Holland, my passport details were copied by Dutch military police and ended up in my local police station in Belfast where my father spotted them. So much for the free world.

The Italian electrician and myself went ashore the next night and tried the next night club on the block. Like the other one it was a huge amphitheatre of a place, but less expensive and certainly more friendly. Soon we were chatting to two women from Amsterdam whose presence in Rotterdam was a bit of a mystery. They both spoke perfect English, and one was a dark haired girl of Armenian descent who took an instant liking to our Italian electrician who shared her southern European good looks. They could not stay on in the club with us, they told us, as they had other arrangements made, but would see us next day at the landing stage and show us round Rotterdam. We took our leave of them and went back to the ship well pleased with our meeting, and looking forward to wholesome female company the next day.

Next day on board there was the usual sharing of experiences of the previous night's carousel, with much embellishment of course. The electrician, who spoke Greek as well as English, was privy to the doings of the engine room staff, most of whom had no English.

Apparently the third and fourth engineers had been ashore during the day and had met two presentable prostitutes in a restaurant. They arranged to sleep with them later that night for quite a sum of guilders, and so it happened. The fourth engineer was very swarthy, had a twisted leg and also had furiously crossed eyes. With his pencil moustache and limping gait he looked positively villainous, although, as he had no English, I have no idea what his character was like. I did know, however, that his table manners were disgusting as he had turned my stomach many a time by blowing his nose on a paper napkin and depositing it in his used coffee cup. The third engineer was small and squat with Negroid features and crinkly hair. Again, as he never spoke either Greek or English to me, I have no idea what his character was like. Anyway the electrician had seen the photograph of the two Dutch girls they had slept with and they were the same two we had to meet in the afternoon for sightseeing. Both the electrician and myself were mortified, gutted, horrified, as well as disappointed. We were of course as jealous as hell, but decided to keep the date and say nothing of our unfortunate discovery.

The two girls met us as arranged at the landing stage. They were modestly dressed and my companion, whose name was Gretaminke, wore no make-up, was bright of eye and soft of speech. She was tall, willowy and blond, with aquiline features, grey eyes and had a smile that illuminated her whole face. She was an intelligent, good looking girl who looked what she said she was, the daughter of an Amsterdam bourgeois who worked in her father's firm. We went to parks, museums, saw Rotterdam's famous buildings, and had afternoon tea in the genteel Boerscafe, with its string ensemble playing Mozart and Vivaldi. There is a convention about sailors that they talk about women on the ship and talk about ships in the brothel, but our conversation ran the whole gamut of the human condition. Indeed it was an innocent and eddifying afternoon. Later we had a meal in a modest restaurant and, all in all, we spent less money than we would have if we had no female company. I banished the thought of the uncouth and ferociously ugly fourth engineer from my mind, willing him away with the thought that Antonio the Italian had been mistaken, but unfortunately the timing of our companions' departure the previous evening tied in with the engineers' story. During the meal Tony or Adonis, as the Greeks called him, raised the question of where the two girls were staying in Rotterdam, as it was rather late for a journey back to Amsterdam. They assured us they had private accommodation and we were invited to go back with them. We took a taxi to a part of the city where there were six story blocks of workers' flats.

They were post war buildings, grim but not forbidding. Each window was fitted with a mirror so the occupants could watch the street without getting up. On the second floor we pressed the bell of an apartment and were immediately ushered into a scene of domesticity with a working class family of two adults and two children seated round a T.V. set. It was a very domestic scene, yet the man when he got up made no effort to introduce himself to us and the girls, who obviously knew the family made no greeting except to say hello to the man who merely opened the doors of two bedrooms which opened off the living room. I realised immediately that there was a commercial arrangement between these girls and the tenant of the flat. I knew also that my worst fears were correct, that the story of the third and fourth engineers was correct, and that these two very respectable looking young women were in fact prostitutes who had a private arrangement with the tenant of a council flat to entertain their clients. My first thought was for the children. What sort of a father would allow prostitutes to use the family home? Anyway we all went into the one room without comment and then the girls went out to get coffee. Tony's first words were, 'This is going to cost us money'. I was too confused even to think about it as I had developed a strong feeling for Gretaminka which was now being engulfed by feelings of doubt, jealousy and distress.

The girls came back with coffee and assured us that this was where they stayed when they visited Rotterdam and that the family did not mind if they brought their friends back. As so often in life, I found myself believing what I wanted to believe, even though all my instincts and common sense told me that it was not true. Tony and the other girl said their goodnights and disappeared into the other room and then Gretaminka undressed without embarrassment. As if reading my thoughts she said, 'I am only doing this because I love you', and I believed her. Our lovemaking was more affectionate than erotic, sacred rather than profane, and accompanied by many tender expressions of love in the Dutch language which I can remember to this day. The next morning Gretaminka rose and brought coffee and rolls to the room where we were joined by Tony and the Armenian girl.

As the electrician had to be on standby for the winches, we got a taxi to the landing stage after agreeing to see the girls later that evening. Tony told me that the question of payment for services never arose with the Armenian girl and his mind seemed more focused on his financial good fortune than on the character of the girl. We met as arranged later that evening at the landing stage where I was presented with a pair of socks and a box of chocolates, which touched me deeply. My mind was in a turmoil with feelings of love and affection, interrupted by the awful image of the Quasimodo-like third engineer paying his money over and the lovely Gretaminka submitting to his embraces. We spent another pleasant evening together at the night club and later returned to the Dutch family's apartment. Once together there was a bond between us which dispelled all doubts, a veil was drawn over all the areas of past history and present occupations, except perhaps my present occupation as a Radio Officer on a Greek ship, which seemed to Gretaminka to be a bit incongrous.

We sailed the next day for Peru and I never saw her again, but I received a letter in Panama, couched in tender language, but with no mention of the everyday aspects of life and small talk with which we normally fill out a letter. My own letter, posted in Panama, elicited no reply and, when next in Rotterdam, I phoned the number she gave me but she was no longer there. Whore or no, she was a wonderful, tender human being and I hope she landed on her feet. Sometimes I would look across the mess table to the third engineer and would be glad he had no English and that I had no Greek.

The life at sea, with its routine of watchkeeping, traffic lists, position reports, alternating with mealtimes watching the same faces across the table, with the predictable menu according to the day, and the half understood conversations in Greek, becomes very irksome when one's thoughts are with someone ashore. With time the routine and the boredom become soporific as the endless vista of sea becomes shorter in miles on the chart, and eventually the spirit rises as the prospect of landfall becomes imminent. I was very aware of the old maxim that a day at sea was a day wasted and tried to occupy my time learning German with the aid of a primer and the letters from Poland. There was a sailor on board who had pidgin German, dating from the German occupation of Greece, and who would chatter away to me but he would soon run out of words and I doubt if he understood half of what I said. The Captain and his wife would sometimes come into the radio room and talk history and politics and through them I became quite well educated in contempory Greek life. The most consoling thought of all was the thought of the dollars mounting up in the Seamen's Savings Bank in New York.

San Juan loading ore was routine, but this time we had orders for Emden in Germany, which pleased everybody except the electrician and myself who had been hoping for Rotterdam again. No more letters had come from that scource so I resigned myself to closing a happy chapter in life, a bright flame that had faltered and died because the fuel of togetherness had ceased, leaving a void which would be sad for a while but which eventually would fill.

The voyage across the Atlantic was uneventful until about five days out from Panama when a force eleven hurricane hit us. The noise of the wind was horrendous, the low lying and elongated T2 was often submerged except for the bridge and afterdeck. Some of the sailors and firemen could be seen praying in corners. I could only hope that the naval architects who designed the elongation of the ship had got their sums right. A Mayday call was broadcast over the Portishead radio scheduled traffic list which was most unusual. Apparently a transatlantic airliner had engine trouble half way over the Atlantic and ships were asked to keep a look out.

The mate on watch reported a low flying aircraft which again was most unusual as planes flew at thirty thousand feet over the Atlantic. I reported this to Portishead and stayed on watch in case there were any developments. The waves were now breaking over the bridge and I knew that if the plane came down it would be impossible to pick up any survivors. I had to wedge my legs against the legs of the desk to stop myself from being flung from my seat. All the loose objects such as books, pencils, spare headphones and such were being flung from one part of the radio room to the other. We went for meals through a tunnel under the deck but the cooks could only manage hot tea and sandwiches. There are bars which can be put up round the stoves in the galley but the pots were being tumbled out of these, so all cooking had to be abandoned. Eventually a message went out that the crippled plane had landed safely at Shannon so I could close the station and go to bed. The waves which were thundering against my port hole were about forty foot higher than the deck. This had never happened before and made me apprehensive.

However I had been on watch for ten hours, was exhausted by the extra movements neccessary to stay upright and fell into a deep sleep. Even through the deep sleep I could hear the roar of the storm.

Next morning our ship was still lurching and pitching, the noise of the wind was frightening, but another sound of crashing and banging filled the air. I looked out and the water was crashing against the port hole, a frightening forty foot from the deck, but when it receded I could see hanging from the davitts splintered matchwood where our thirty foot lifeboat should have been. The force of the waves smashing against the midships had demolished it completely and yet it had been a solidly clinker built vessel passed by the insurance for survival in the western ocean.

I was now able to pick up the Irish radio and could listen to the news broadcasts of the details of the storm damage ashore. Now that a third of the lifesaving capacity was gone it brought it home to me that I had never had a boat drill in any ship since I left the Mac Andrew ship when we found that the lifeboat was rusted on to the deck. In a force eleven hurricane there would be no chance of successfully launching a lifeboat but in the case of a collision or explosion it is vital that the deck crew know exactly where to go and what to do.

The storm abated as we entered the English Channel and we soon were anchored off the island of Borkum a few miles out in the estuary of the river Ems which forms the border between Holland and Germany. I received a signal from Nordeich radio that we would have to wait a couple of days for an empty berth in Emden and we were all surprised when a launch full of German shipyard workers pulled alongside. The workmen climbed aboard, went down into the engine room and started pulling out heater pipes in the oil storage tanks. None of them could speak English so the chief engineer, who resented my presence on board, was forced to ask me to translate for him. Apparently the job had been booked in to the shipyard on our E.T A. date and when we didn't arrive they came out to look for us so as not to loose time.

The engine room was situated under the sailors' mess where there was a non-stop coffee urn for the benefit of the crew coming on and off watch. The German engine gang soon discovered this and would pop up for a coffee when they had a chance. I talked to one of them and he told me his foreman was a 'Sklavtreiber' (slavedriver). Later when we docked, the police were to come on board and insist on the coffee urn being closed down at the behest of the shipyard employers. This meant that our crew were also deprived of their coffee, and it seemed to me that it was none of the business of the Germans but apparently the law was on their side.

It was good to see a few more faces around and to be able to converse, and listen to, a language other than Greek. The Suez invasion by the British and French took place just at this time and the whole ship became reliant on me for news which I got via the B.B.C. overseas and which was remarkably objective. The Greeks instinctively were on the side of the Egyptians, some of them thought that the third world war would break out and made their way to the Captain's cabin to sign off. The Germans told me that old laid-up merchant vessels were being re-commissioned as freight rates had rocketed. It made me wonder if Goulandris had prior knowledge of British /French/ Israeli war plans as they had booked in our vessel for oil tank pipe renewal some time before the conflict began. The electrician who lived in Egypt was less worried than the Greeks and he sided with the invasion coalition. He doubted that the Egyptians would be able to run the Canal on their own, but then the Soviet Union agreed to send them skilled navigators thus invalidating that argument. Anyway, the invasion succeeded in closing the Canal so oil had to be taken round the Cape, resulting in a fifty percent more carrying capacity requirement. Consequently freight rates doubled and the shipowners who had spare tonnage, like Goulandris with their dual purpose ships, made a fortune. When we did dock at the port of Emden we could see shipyard men scurrying over old vessels which were being made ready to take advantage of the shipping shortage.

Our own vessel's heating pipe renewal continued at the quayside to enable us to go to Maracaibo in Venezuela to take on an oil cargo for the United States. A lot of crew changes took place in Emden, as the Suez crisis was still raging, and the ones who feared a war and took repatriation had to be replaced. Our Captain was transferred to another ship in the U.S., causing a void in both friendship and leadership in my life as he had been the only one in my seafaring career who shared an interest with me in politics, history and literature. A strong democrat, a cultured and intelligent man, Captain Campanis had been thoughtful enough to realise that the isolation of my position needed extra companionship and he provided it. His replacement was the opposite, a brash philistine, a Greek who lived in the United States and had contempt for his fellow countrymen. I was to have more contact with him than most when we were at sea as I had to handle his messages to and from the shipowners and I did not relish it.

Emden was a town rather than a city and it was small enough to get to know most pubs and restaurants there in a couple of nights. The town had been completely rebuilt after massive damage by allied bombers in the war but retained the typical German architecture which, unlike the British post war development, gave the place atmosphere. I found an interesting 'Kneipe' or pub where a three piece ensemble played Viennese waltzes interspersed with oompah marches and the odd folk tune. Some of the locals would play cards, as they do in the country pubs in Ireland, while the young people would sing and dance to the music. A seafaring town, everybody had a friend or relative 'seeleute' and their first question would be 'Was machen sie an board?' 'What's your job on board?'. One evening I went to a Kneipe, which I found convivial, where I was greeted by a notice which said 'World Cup Match admission 2 marks'. It was still the era when you had to be moderately rich to own a T.V. set and the pub was showing the quarter finals between West Germany and, would you believe, Northern Ireland. The pub was crowded and even the very earnest card players had abandoned their game to cheer for Germany. Never having much interest in sport I was completely unaware of Northern Ireland's success in soccer but I found myself getting excited and cheering our successes in the match. This brought a few dirty looks from the Germans and I felt obliged to say to nobody in particular 'Ich bin Nordirlander'. This molified them all somewhat and I was allowed to cheer our team's victory over the Bundesrepublik.

Another night I went to the pub with the ensemble where I had a drink with two of the apprentices who were pleased to practise their English. It was coming up near Christmas, the bunting and fairy lights were up and it was Friday night. Our ship was now the only one in port apart from a German coaster, whose crew were carousing at the bar. Glasses of schnapps were being tossed back to shouts of 'Bravo Zimmerman' and it transpired that it was the carpenter's birthday. A young woman amongst three sitting next to us asked me in English if we were off a British ship and it transpired that she was married to an English bosun. Her two companions had no English but I managed to converse in German with her sister who worked in the bar beside the dock gate. She was a pretty blond girl, tall, blue-eyed, lithe, and with a sense of humour. She doubled up with laughter as she told me that I had come into her bar earlier and attempted to talk to the owner's Alsation dog in German using the respectful form 'Sie' instead of the familiar form 'Du'. We have no equivalent in English, but I suppose it would be the same as addressing a dog as 'My dear fellow'.

    I left Sophie back to her parent's house that night and discovered that my German learnt from a book could be understood, and found also that although Sophie rattled on as if I were a native speaker I could always get the gist of what she was saying. We met every night for meals in small restaurants or went to the cinema and from her I learnt of the difficulties of growing up in devastated post war Germany. Her father had been a customs officer and had been arrested and interned as soon as the British army crossed the border from Holland. Although he had been a member of the Social Democrats prewar, because he had been wearing a uniform, he was locked up. She also told me that the mayor of the town had been a Nazi but either the British had overlooked this or he had managed to cover his tracks. We went to the cinema one night where they were showing a Finnish Film dubbed in German called the 'Unknown Soldier'. This concerned the war between Finland and the Soviet Union in 1941 over Karelia. The film made the point that Karelia was inhabited by Karelians on both sides of the border and that war was unnecessary, pointless and cruel. Another film we went to see was 'Moby Dick', an American film about the great whale. It was also dubbed in German and to my astonishment a local actor from Belfast's Group Theatre appeared apparently spouting German for all he was worth. Another evening I was walking Sophie home when a small group of people passed on the other side of the nearly deserted street. Sophie said to me in a low voice 'Sie Sind Katolisch'. 'They are Catholics', she said in such a way that I was expected to understand the significance of her observation, which I took to mean that Catholics were viewed with suspicion in this part of Protestant North Germany. It reminded me of being on the Castlereagh Road in Belfast as a child when another child pointed to the four Catholic people who were returning from mass and said exactly the same thing.

    As our cargo was fast being unloaded, a leaden feeling of forboding enshrouded my being, as the thought of leaving this friendly German town where I felt so much at home. Sophie's mother was ill with leukaemia which meant that we had no place to shelter with our trysts so I suggested she come back to the ship where we would be undisturbed in my well heated accommodation. Reluctantly she agreed to this knowing that we would soon be sailing. We arrived by taxi after a meal ashore and left instructions for the taxi driver to pick her up about eleven at night. No sooner had we our coats off when we heard the engines starting up and felt the ship move away from the quay. I rushed up to the bridge meaning to arrange with the pilot to take Sophie back on the pilot launch, as I thought we must be finished unloading and now on our way to Panama.

The new Captain was on the bridge and he told me we were just moving out to sea for the night and returning to the shipyard in the morning to complete the work on the heater pipes. I had not realised that the new Captain did not automatically inform me of the ship's movements the way Captain Campanis did but did realise that he probably would not be pleased to know that I had a girl on board so I kept quiet about that. Anyway, Sophie was pleased to learn that she was not on her way to South America but she was worried about her mother wondering where she was. The night at sea passed pleasantly enough, the noise of the engines woke us up in time to get dressed and ready for shore. We slipped down the gangplank as soon as it was lowered, congratulating ourselves that the shipyard had not yet started and Sophie would be home before breakfast. The taxi we had ordered the previous night pulled up. The driver was determined not to let his bone go with the dog and had found out that the ship was booked into the shipyard and had turned up to collect his fare.

CAPTAIN QUEEG, THE GREEK

The Nordseewerke finished the repairs to the oiltank heater pipes in two days and we were on our way again, this time as an oil tanker rather than a bulk carrier. There were rumours emanating from the deck department that the new Captain with his American-born wife had instituted an iron regime on the bridge. I was now twenty-four years old and had enough sea miles under my belt under different flags to exhibit a self-confidence that affected the new Captain's attitude to me. I was rather surprised however that he phrased all his telegrams in Greek, presumably so that I would not be privy to their contents. This posed difficulties, both for myself and the American coast stations, as it was always uncertain whether the spelling was correct or not, and inevitably there had to be requests for repeats. The Captain's wife was an attractive middle-aged woman and naturally she would talk to me as we were the only native English speakers on board. However, if he saw her talking to me he would shout at her in Greek and she would have to go back to his cabin. There were quite a few new faces on board, replacement crew for the ones who had paid off and gone back to Greece.

Amongst them was a red haired officer's steward who was continually sea sick, and as we were light ship he never got a chance to find his sea legs as the ship was tossing about without a regular rhythm. He had worked ashore in Greece in a munitions factory making bazookas and had been paid off due to the fact that Greece had joined N.A.T.O. and now had to use American bazookas. His pay on board was £30 a month all found, while before it had been about ten pounds, so naturally he was keen to do well and keep his job so he struggled manfully on. Manolis, the third mate, had been promoted second mate and a new third mate arrived. He was a very different type of Greek seafarer as he was only about twenty-two, spoke fluent English, was obviously well educated, the middle-class product of the new post war Greek society that looked to Britain and America rather than the old Greek values. I noticed that he did not talk much to Manolis the proud Cretan, and made fun to me of the older Aegean sailors. One day the chief steward said to me 'Capitanos iss crazy man!' The Captain had been complaining about his food in his curt imperious way that had denied the playing out of the traditional Greek pantomine.

The temperamental steward simply withdrew into himself and said 'I say nothing but I leave ship in United States. You and me both Marconi, we get other job.' I gathered from this that the Captain had been complaining about me to the steward, which surprised me as I prided myself on my efficiency at my job. This did not bother me unduly as most deck people had only a very hazy idea about what the job entailed and as long as the captains got weather reports and telegrams received and transmitted promptly they generally left the Radio Officer to get on with it.

The last day we had been in Emden I had been coming back to the ship in the gathering gloom of the winter evening when I came on a chain across the quay. The notice by its side warned of the danger of approaching ships. What it meant was that the iron jetty retracted into itself in a sort of maritime level crossing to let small vessels enter the inner harbour without going out into the estuary. I saw the approaching coaster and reckoned there would be a five minute wait for the operation to be over. Impatiently I jumped over the chain and started to walk over the retractable section when it started to move backwards into the wall of the jetty. The coaster was fast approaching the opening as I could see the man on the foreward bow and hear the noise of its wake. On pure reflex I jumped the three feet or more to the other side as the coaster passed through the entrance. I knew I was dead if I didn't make it as the coaster must have been doing a good eight knots and I thought of the after life and decided there was none, and it was best to stay alive. These thoughts raced through my mind as I grabbed the chain and hauled myself to safety at the other side. Ever since I have considered myself an atheist with the philosophy that religion chains men's minds, cripples scientific thought and undermines self confidence.

Now out at sea in a lull in the west Atlantic winter storm, I was walking back from the officers' mess in the stern section to the bridge amidships when a freak wave crashed over the deck and lifted me off my feet. I could see the Captain's wife standing on the veranda deck looking aft, so I shouted out. The ship lurched upwards to free itself fron the weight of water on its deck and I was caught in the down tow as the water flowed over the side. I grabbed the iron rail and hung on for dear life until the water cleared itself and again considered myself lucky to be alive. I was soaked through with freezing water and rushed under the hot shower before taking off my clothes. I looked into the chart room where the second mate Manolis was on watch and told him what had happened.

He told me that the Captain's wife had rushed up to the chart room shouting that Marconi had gone over board. The Captain, who was studying the chart, only looked up to say, 'If you can't be quiet go down to the cabin' and continued to peruse the chart. It was then that I realized that we were not sailing under a fully sane Captain.

Ten days later we approached a sea of light that was the bay of Maracaibo in Venezuela. The bay itself had a narrow entrance but broadened out to an area of several hundred square miles, all of which was illuminated by gas flares from off-shore oil rigs. I had not given much thought to this country, which for me was unusual as I liked to find out as much as possible about a new landfall. The chief mate said that it was the most expensive country in the world and there his store of knowledge finished. The previous Captain had an encyclopaedic knowledge, political, demographic and economic, of every place we visited, but this new man was far too flaky to converse with. Indeed his eccentricity was such that I found my thoughts centred solely on the ship and its running.

The pilot came on board and per usual was an U.S. educated South American with perfect English. As usual I went up to the bridge for a chat as I could justify my presence there in case the pilot wanted communication with the shore. Anyway, he had a personal very high frequency set linked to his office so my services were unneccessary. Idly chatting he asked me if I had ever been before in Maracaibo or did I know any one there. Only at that moment did I remember that my cousin Maureen from Cheltenham had got a job with the Royal Dutch Shell company and that her place of work was in Maracaibo. Why I had not thought of it before I don't know, perhaps the on board tensions had driven it from my mind. The pilot said 'Well Sparks, that is where you are going to, Camp O'Reilly operated by Royal Dutch Shell.' He radioed in to his office with a message for Miss Maureen King to say her cousin would be arriving on the Andros Saturn at the oil jetty in an hour's time. I had spent the weekend at my aunt's house in Cheltenham before joining Marconi in Liverpool, and Maureen had already got the job then, but over the years I had lost contact. I had been sent to primary school in Cheltenham away from the family, for what reason I don't know, and Maureen had always corresponded with my brother when he was in the army, and indeed he spent weekends with the Kings when stationed in England.

Anyway, as fate would have it, I had landed up on Maureen's doorstep in Venezuela in the course of my work. We docked in the bright tropical afternoon as an open-topped Volkswagen parked on the oil jetty. Sure enough, my cousin Maureen and another blond girl waved up to me and they came aboard as soon as the gangplank went down. The sailors and firemen as usual lined the rail to break the boredom of the voyage and I heard the sotto voice remark 'Puste Ihnne' pass between them. They obviously thought I had ordered up two prostitutes by radio, although how they thought I managed to find two fair-haired, blue-eyed prostitutes in Venezuela escapes me. My cousin was delighted to see me and her friend was a fellow teacher from the oil company school. They had been in Venezuela for two years, taught children of Venezuelan, British, American and Dutch parents through the medium of English. I arranged for the steward to serve tea and sandwiches but when he came to the cabin he leered at the girls and for a moment I thought he was going to ask them their fee. I explained that one was my cousin but he just went away laughing. I looked up at the porthole and saw a trio of moustachioed grinning faces looking in, obviously expecting a voyeuristic experience. When we went ashore I think the whole ship's crew was lining the rails, grinning lasciviously.

    I spent the next two days in the air conditioned luxury of my cousin's bungalow where she had the services of a Venezuelan maid, a lovely Indian girl whose only fault was that she kept getting pregnant, obliging my cousin to look after her during and after her pregnancy. The headmaster of the oil company school was a Trelew Argentinian who spoke fluent Welsh and Spanish but alas no English. He was a descendant of the hardy Welsh dissidents who made a Welsh-speaking colony in Argentina at the latter end of the last century.

    Maracaibo was a flourishing expensive modern town with white villas, bougainvillaea, neon lights and American cars. I was able to travel around the flat countryside outside the city with my cousin. I could see the usual South American shanties on sugar plantations, but every five miles or so we would pass a corrugated iron palisade fence enclosing about an acre of land. The fencing would always be about ten feet high and would bear the legend 'Country Dancing' written in letters two feet tall. My cousin told me these were brothels which theoretically were illegal, but the euphemism 'country dancing' had been universally adopted and as long as the fences were high enough to hide the real activity taking place the policia left them alone. The time was just before Christmas so I was invited to the school concert which was a delightful affair held in the open air. Groups of infants sang carols in English, Spanish and Dutch, and even acted out nativity plays using the three languages. At the time I thought that if only our schools would teach infants foreign languages as soon as they start school it would obviate the tedium of learning foreign language grammar at a later date. Christmas carols in the tropics under the moonlight, with a gentle cooling breeze stirring the palm fronds, was an experience so far removed from the world of ships and seamen, it was hard to realise that the oil jetty with the Andros Saturn moored alongside was just down the road.

We sailed the next day for Perth Amboy in the state of New Jersey but within the outer reaches of New York harbour, and within four short days, the weather had changed from tropical to continental ice and snow. We moored alongside an oil refinery on Christmas morning, and a right miserable Christmas day it proved to be. The engineers were all down in the engine room trying to unfreeze the heavy oil cargo which had thickened so much in the sub-zero temperature that it would not flow. The steward had not arranged anything special except a bottle of beer and the Captain left immediately for his home in New York City. The snow was scudding across New York harbour as I went ashore in Perth Amboy to explore the town. There was a long main street of single-story wooden buildings punctuated by blinking neon signs. The street was deserted except for one or two large cars full of children clutching Christmas toys. An odd couple were to be seen scurrying through the snow, obviously on their way to in-laws for the festivities. I passed a confectioner/newspaper shop and noted that it had as many Polish language newspapers as English. On the outskirts of the town there was the usual supermarket with its car park, fast food place, both of which were closed. I made my way through the snow back to the ship and went to bed with a book. I remembered the last Christmas I spent at sea where the captain gave a dinner party and the crew staged a review, but then I remembered that the Greeks made a much bigger event at Easter time when painted eggs were cracked and toasts drunk. Perth Amboy was about an hour's train ride from New York, so next day I boarded the quaintly old fashioned New Jersey Railway which brought me to Grand Central Station in Manhattan. New York, as bustling and exciting as ever, was a tonic after the dreariness of our landfall in Perth Amboy.

I went straight to the King Edward Hotel in Forty Seventh Street and booked into a room. This was the Hotel which housed the British Merchant Navy Officers' Club which was a residual welfare institution dating from the second world war. During the war the Atlantic convoys assembled in New York harbour for the perilous journey to Britain so there would be thousands of British seamen ashore in New York and at a loose end. The Club was set up and film and show business stars would appear to entertain the M.N. officers and, as a result, a considerable amount of money was collected and the club continued after the war on the surplus profits. The steward of the Club was a friendly Scot who put me right about many aspects of life in New York and on hearing my accent told me of the Belfast man who was port captain of the United Fruit Company. I contacted this person on the phone and he told me he would give me the first radio officer's job that became vacant in his company if I was on the spot at the time. I was to telephone Captain Brown every time I was in the United States, without result, until one last night in New York before returning home, a vacancy occurred on a ship in Baton Rouge, Louisiana. I agonised whether to continue my seafaring career at American rates of pay, or to resume a settled life at home with my Polish bride-to-be. I chose the latter which did not occur as planned, but that's another story for another day.

The M.N. Officers Club was the gathering place for British expatriots in New York where they could drink subsidised liquor and operate an employment network such as I have described. There were some Northern Ireland girls there who were nurses, earning much better money than they would at home because of the cash nexus of the American hospitals, where the insurance companies pay all the expenses and those without insurance or money literally die. While I was at Perth Amboy I escorted some of the crew to the U.S. Public Health Hospital on Staten Island. I found that these hospitals were run by the U.S. Navy, that is, staffed by navy surgeons, nurses, sick berth ratings, etc. These hospitals were free to merchant seamen and from what I could gather people without health insurance could get treatment free as well. There were lots of poor blacks and Puerto Ricans in the corridors, often getting consultations from the navy doctors in front of everybody. I wonder did Franklin Roosevelt use his authority as Commander-in-Chief of the armed forces to institute this rudimentary health service over the objections of the medical lobby.

We loaded light oil to take to Argentina, back into the warm weather and settled down to the routine of watchkeeping, when I seemed to develope a slight gastric 'flu. Normally my watchkeeping times varied with the time zones and in this part of the world the first watch started at 6 a.m. This morning I decided to stay on in bed to help get over the bug and, as most Captians would not know or bother about my watchkeeping times which were denoted in Greenwich Mean Time rather than local time, I did not bother to tell anyone. There were no weather reports or traffic lists broadcast in the early watch so there was nothing lost. However, our Greek Captain Queeg apparently sent the third mate down to the radio room every morning to see if I was on watch so I was summoned to the chart room to face a charge. I was nonplussed as an officer to be logged meant the end of his career and I explained that I was sick, but to no avail. The man seemed to revel in making trouble, so I realised that drastic measures would have to be used to make him see sense.

Under the Liberian articles (which were a straight copy of the American ones) a seaman could pay off in any port in the world, so I told him that I would leave the ship in Buenos Aires and go home D.B.S. (distressed British seaman). I knew that the company would be obliged to find another R.O. in New York or even London and fly him out to Argentina, which could cause them hundreds of dollars in fares and possibly thousands of dollars in delayed sailing. To be at odds with one's immediate boss is an unnerving situation, but to have tension on board ship is completely demoralising, so I relaxed when I came to terms with the fact that I would leave the ship at Buenos Aires, and even looked forward to having a holiday there before returning home. I confided in the second mate, Manolis, who knew what victimisation was, having served five penal years in the Greek army for his father's patriotism. He informed me that the skipper had victimised him for some minor matter but he would wait until we reached the States again before he paid off, which was sensible as Buenos Aires was not the place to find another job.

I knew in the nature of things that Manolis would tell a confidante in the crew of my resolution to pay off and eventually it would get back to the Skipper but my mind was made up and I did not care. A loud morse signal let me know there was another ship nearby, so I called him up on 500 kcs. As luck would have it, he was coming from the same place for which we were bound, and he told me we would lighten ship at Ricolada Island before heading up the River Plate and then the Parana River. I will never forget Ricolada, indeed the name is etched on my psyche as the place where we steamed past the pilot on the luckless ship Micape.

Apparently the ship lightening procedure took place outside the three mile limit and it was quite legal to sell duty-free American cigarettes to the crews of the oil barges. I did not smoke but I drew several thousand cigarettes from the steward and imparted this intelligence to the electrician and the second mate. When we anchored alongside the oil barges off Ricolada, I was surprised to see the winches being operated in preparation for unloading. To everyone's surprise, boxes of cartoned cigarettes were being unloaded on to the oil barges while the oil was being pumped into them. These belonged to the Captain who must have placed a huge order for duty-free before sailing. Our Captain had obviously been here before and was selling the ship's bond at an enormous profit quite legally. An Argentine gunboat lay off at about half a mile and I suppose the Captain would move in on the oil barge crews if they didn't pay him off. We unloaded sufficient oil to raise the freeboard enough to travel up the Parana River, which forms the border between Argentina and Paraguay, and so set off on a trip which was to take us steaming past the magnificent waterfronts of Buenos Aires and five hundred miles into the pampas. Before this happened the Captain's quiet American wife appeared in my cabin bearing a tray of Greek sweetmeats and a glass of ouzo. She expressed her husband's felicitations and assured me I would get to see a doctor as soon as we docked. I had won the war of nerves and this was his peace offering, gratefully accepted I might add, as I had no desire to be adrift in Buenos Aires with my name in the ship's log.

We took on board no less than 4 river pilots to make the five hundred mile journey upstream to the oil refinery. Apparently each pilot had to be watched by another pilot in case the ship was run aground as an act of economic sabotage which would close the river to navigation. The land on either bank was flat, scrubby, and devoid of any sign of human habitation as far as the eye could see, causing me to wonder why so many people in the world were going hungry with so much good, well watered land lying fallow. After a day and a night, we steamed past wooden shacks, little patches of cultivated land, and the odd orchard which appeared on the Argentine side, heralding the nearness of the cowboy town where we docked.

When we did dock, I had occasion to collect a visa and the address of the local doctor from the office of the oil refinery manager. His Argentine citizenship certificate adorned the wall bearing the name Horatio O'Meara and indeed he turned out to be an Irishman from Co. Meath in the service of Shell Oil. Mr O'Meara had lived in this literal backwater for twenty years and had been obliged to take Argentine citizenship and change his first name to Horatio from Harold to conform with the law which stated that only Spanish Christian names could be given. 'It's much the same as Athlone', he said, which is also a bit of a backwater.

The town itself was made up largely of wooden shacks, with rails to tie up horses, but there was something quiet and eerie about it. There was not the same noise and bustle as the port of Engineiro White where I had spent the last memorable New Year's Eve. Then I realised what the difference was. All the people were sitting in serried ranks, on chairs on the side walk, watching television sets mounted on the walls outside the cafes. Television had come to Argentina since my last visit.

I found a bar with German gothic letters on the outside so I asked for a drink in German. The youth behind the bar was tall, blond and blue eyed, but the rough wooden floor, the delapidated flyblown curtains and a general air of decay belied the connection with the Fatherland. The lad spoke fluent German and told me he was the grandchild of the original settlers who came from Bavaria at the turn of the century to be apple growers. Most of the people in the area were of German descent and engaged in fruit growing, but the markets were distant and the prices bad, so the young people generally left to seek their fortunes in Buenos Aires or Cordoba. I thought of the gleaming new buildings in Emden and Bremen, the spotlessly clean and modern restaurants and bars and wondered why did people travel to the other end of the earth to seek their fortune. Perhaps to avoid the wars that plagued Europe, but South America has not been the most peaceful continent.

The Captain arranged a consultation with a local doctor, who turned out to be an Italian, who sounded my chest by putting his ear to it without benefit of stethoscope. My constant diarrhoea was being caused by greasy Greek food so he gave me tablets and put me on a diet. The diet was milk-and fat-free, so I could look forward, in a situation where eating was the only pleasure, to vegetables and black tea. Walking back to the ship down the dusty road to the muddy Parana I met some of the crew. The pumpman, who was a grizzled ancient mariner with a row of gold teeth, cross eyes and a pencilled moustache, had bought a gold ring. 'Zeste', he said, drawing his hand across his brow. Zeste, Greek for hot, and the action of showing his new gold ring as he mopped his brow, raised a chuckle from his companions, in which I joined.

Suddenly I became weak and depressed as I realised that for the past three years I had missed out on the cut and thrust of humourous banter which is the leaven of the staff of life. Here I was at the age of twenty-four in a dusty backwater in the Argentine pampas, without people who spoke my language, and with nothing before me but the sight of the sea and a diet of black tea and vegetables. The energy drain and depression I now know was the onset of Myalgic Encephalomyelitis from which I now chronically suffer, but at that time was unknown except as the 'Royal Free Disease' which infected all the staff of the Royal Free Hospital in London in 1955. I struggled back to the ship and went to bed, sleeping the sleep of the exhausted with the attendant bizarre dreams that accompany this devastating condition. Luckily my job was not physically or mentally onerous and I had every opportunity of healing sleep, and, being young and fit, I shook it off in the following weeks on our trip through the Magellan Straits. In later life I was not so fortunate as I have now been handicapped by this condition for the last nine years.

On the voyage down the Argentine coast we were accompanied by a pilot who took us through the narrow channels of the Magellan Straits which separate Tierra del Fuega from the South American mainland. In the old days of sail the windjammers had to go round the stormy Cape Horn, as there is no wind in the Straits, enclosed as they are by massive mountains. Indeed the Straits are so narrow in some parts that there was barely room for the ship to pass. It reminded me of the Highlands of Scotland with the sound of the ship's engines echoing through the still hills and the wild deer at the water's edge scattering at the noise. Indeed it was eerie with not a sign of a human being the whole passage.

The eerieness was reflected in the radio room where the only signal was the weak reedy morse from Punta Arenas Chilean Navy station, giving a sense of isolation. I imagined some lonely trapper tramping through this landscape, lighting a campfire in the solitude and then hearing the thump-thump-thump of the ship's engines disturbing his solitude. Into the Pacific Ocean, steaming up the Chilean coast, the warming sun lifted our spirits, so much so that the fourth engineer would sing and play his guitar on the fantail in the heel of the evening. There was a strange atmosphere on board, due, I believe, to the odd eccentric behaviour of the Captain. We had all been at sea a long time, in my case fifteen months, but the Greeks seldom left a ship except to go home, and I discovered that most of the crew were paying off as soon as we got to either Europe or the U.S. An unhappy ship is one where the Captain's personality is not in tune with the crew and I discovered that the usual Greek way of arguing, that is shouting at the top of one's voice, had no place in the scheme of things with this Captain. He issued edicts and refused to argue and threatened to sack anyone who gainsaid him. The crew were uneasy and they were prepared to lose wages and take their chance on another ship.

I awoke one morning in the bright sunlight and colourful surroundings of Valparaiso, looking out on the grey hull of a warship called the O'Brien. This arrested my attention as O'Brien is my middle name, called after Lord Inchquin, who had some vague connection with my mother's family. I remembered reading that the first president of Chile was called O'Higgins, the son of an Irish pedler, and the pilot told me that an O'Brien was their first admiral. Valparaiso nestled in a bay and its suburbs rose up the sides of a mountain. I dare say it had lovely views of the harbour and the sea, but we were only there to put the pilot ashore and from there he would fly back to Buenos Aires.

We left Valparaiso, steamed peacefully up the Chilean coast until we arrived at a small jetty with one berth which was our loading port. This was a copper mine and an attendant settlement for the miners families, very much like San Juan in Peru, tucked in amongst the sand dunes. This mine apparently was owned by a Hungarian family, and indeed I saw a magnificent woman in jodpurs, standing beside the conveyor belt supervising the loading operation. She was very tall with a venusian figure topped off by a magificent mane of tawney locks. The pilot told me she was the daughter of the family and much sought after by the scions of the Chilean bourgeoisie. The pilot who spoke good English with a strong Brooklyn accent was quite interested in my position on a Greek ship. I explained to him that I earned much more money on this ship and it was worth putting up with the unsocial milieu.

Whether he felt sorry for me because of this or not, I don't know, but he invited me to have dinner with his family that evening. There were some bungalows on the outskirts of the settlement and the pilot lived in one of these surrounded by masses of flowers coaxed to life from the sand by his wife. She also spoke English, being a teacher, as did their charming daughter who was a few years younger than myself and attending the University of Santiago. The meal was mouthwatering and accompanied by a different Chilean wine for every course. My hosts explained to me that Chile was a very civilised and cultured country, much more European than other South American countries and, of course, a democracy in a continent of military dictatorships. They told me of a rancher called Campbell who was an Ulsterman who ran 9,000 acres nearby. I realised that Mr Campbell must have pre-empted the national conflict in Ireland, and so I explained the two nations reality in Ireland to my intrigued hosts. No doubt when this conflict burst on the world scene they could regard themselves as Chilean experts. Their pretty daughter, who was studying English, told me of the idyllic life in the capital where symphony concerts could be heard on balmy evenings in the park, of the broad and leafy boulevards where people strolled in an atmosphere of tranquil contentment. Fuelled by the wine I found that the conversation had been developing into a dialogue between the daughter and myself. I plucked up enough courage to ask the girl to accompany me on a stroll on the beach and, as if by magic, a young girl of about nine years old appeared in the dining room. This was to be our chaperone and she appeared right on cue. She tripped along behind us chattering away in Spanish until we were out of sight of the bungalow when she ran out of sight over the brow of the hill. I gathered this was the time to make my move, so I did. Innocent enough stuff but, for a sailor who had been looking at the sea and little else for many weeks, it was an exciting interlude. The young girl had obviously been coached to stay away long enough for what my companion had in mind and short enough to interrupt the proceedings if nature was beginning to take it's course.

    Anyway, we returned to the house where I made my farewells to a hospitable family of whom I have very fond memories and whom I hope escaped unhurt in the tragedy that overtook their beautiful country in the seventies. Our orders were for the port of Baltimore in the U.S. and it seemed everybody would be paying off, so there was a general lack of interest in the efficiency and well running of the ship. The Captain had alienated even the old chief cook who had been at sea a straight 12 years, and convinced him it was about time he went home, dowries or no dowries.

An uneventful voyage through the Canal, with no stops, and up through the Caribbean, led us to dock in the port of Baltimore. Saying goodbye to my floating home of the past fifteen month's presented no problem, but gathering up and packing fifteen months' accumulated possessions did. Still suffering from stomach upsets, depression and weakness, I decided to visit the famous John Hopkin's Hospital which was also a U.S. public health hospital available for foreign seamen. They took a battery of blood samples and told me to wait for a week for the results so I was obliged to book into a cheap hotel and kick my heels around Baltimore.

The city was old fashioned and reminded me of Belfast, but the only social meeting places I could find were striptease bars. After a while these places become terribly boring, and with my depressed state of mind and the dinginess of the hotel room I found myself just wandering about the streets alone all day until I was tired enough to go back to the hotel and sleep. The results of the blood tests were all negative and I am now convinced that I had a mild dose of the mystifying M.E., which does not show up in the blood but is a very real and distressing physical disease for which there is no cure. It is due to the onset of M.E., in a devasting manner, that I am now able to set down this reminiscence at a very slow pace, at a period when my life should have been at it's Zenith. I met a fellow seaman while waiting at the John Hopkin's Hospital outpatients department. He was American and had visited Belfast and his one abiding memory was the infamous Du Barry's bar where Belfast's few raddled prostitutes used to ply their trade.

I suppose my memories of Baltimore are equally distorted as I just didn't have the energy to find out about the worthwhile places to visit in that city. Anyway, I concluded that there couldn't be anything seriously wrong with me after a thorough examination at a world famous hospital, so I hailed a taxi and set off for the railway station to go to New York. It seemed to be the custom for a cabby to stop along the route to pick up further passengers, which this cabby did. Two elderly women got in, conversing in slightly modified Belfast accents. They turned out be the wife and sister of a Belfast policeman who had emigrated to Baltimore on finishing his service. They had not met anybody from home since settling there and it turned out that they knew my father. Of course I was invited out to their home, but too late. I had spent a demoralising week in a strange city and, in my last minutes there, had met people from home.

NEW YORK, NEW YORK

Orion Shipping had a magnificent suite of offices on Broad Street at the corner of Broadway and Wall Street. Just a few hundred yards away was one of the last nineteenth century red brick buildings, namely the Seamen's Church Mission, which housed up to five hundred seamen in cubicle accommodation at the very affordable price of $1.50 a night. Right in the heart of the financial district, amongst the stockbrokers and bankers, an oasis for seamen of all nationalities existed amongst the most expensive real estate in the world. The 'Doghouse,' as this valuable institution was known, also housed a goodly number of human derelicts, alcoholics and the psychiatrically disturbed. There was a handwritten notice pinned up in the office. It was headed 'Suffering from active T.B. Not to be admitted', and listed the names of about ten people. This sent a shiver down my spine at the thought of men suffering from active T.B wandering the streets of New York and being without shelter in a city where it gets to twenty below in the winter time.

There was a canteen where substantial meals could be had for a very reasonable price, considering it was downtown Manhattan, and it was much patronised by office workers from the great citadels of capitalism nearby. Orion Shipping had a ship arriving in Seattle in a week and asked me to standby for it, so I would have a week's holiday before I joined it. I spent most of my days sightseeing and at night I would go to the British Merchant Navy club and socialise. There was an English R.O who, like myself, was waiting for a job on an American-Greek and he liked the theatre so there was some company for me. Every couple of days I would go to Orion's office to draw some money and, as I had more than a thousand dollars with them, I didn't hesitate to ask. The port captain would get quite angry. He would say, 'You are spending more money than an American family has to keep it for a week.' This made me think that life for the average American was not as rosy as we had been led to believe. I would see my Greek former shipmates there and most of them were also waiting for the ship to arrive in Seattle, and most were discomfited by the lack of shore work available in New York. Most of them had become ensconced in the Greek community in New York which had its own newspaper, football clubs, restaurants and social clubs.

The apprentice, to whom I had been teaching English, had got a job in a car wash but complained about the poor pay and hard work involved. He wanted me to go to 'Athens Corner' for some Greek music and dancing but after fifteen months listening to Greek I preferred to speak English at the M.N. club.

It was refreshing to get up in the morning, have a mug of strong coffee and perhaps some pancakes which the Americans eat, then buy the New York Times which could be read in Battery Park with the salt breeze blowing in from New York harbour, with the Statue of Liberty on the horizon. I returned to this scene thirty years later but the wonderful Seamen's Church Mission had been replaced by three huge skyscrapers and no one in the vicinity had ever heard of it. Such is progress I am told, but what use to society are skyscrapers except for crooks, money manipulators, and economy looters, while the old mission was a home for men who make it all possible by manning the ships that take the world's resources to where they are needed. After a while I got to know some of the more or less permanent residents of the 'Doghouse', and a very interesting bunch they were.

There was a former officer in the navy of the Spanish Republic who had to flee the country when the Fascists won the civil war. He finished up in the Dominican Republic and was made the admiral of their navy. A right wing coup meant that he had again to flee for his life so he found himself in New York looking for a job on a merchant ship. Another long term resident was an American who was an ex-radio officer on the American flag ships which was a very well paid job due mainly to the American R.O's union which was very militant indeed. He was on a cargo ship which traded to Columbia, when he met and fell in love with a Columbian rancher's daughter. He married her, stayed ashore and worked on the ranch with his father-in-law. Again, in Columbia there was a right wing military coup backed by the Catholic church which meant all foreigners who were not of the Catholic faith having to leave the country.

As the American was Jewish he had to leave his wife and family and was told never to come back. It had been seven years since he worked a morse key and his confidence in his ability to do the job had gone, but getting on a ship trading to Columbia was his only chance of seeing his wife and children again. Apparently jobs had come up from time to time but he had panicked at the last minute and turned them down. Perhaps there was another reason for his fear, but knowing of the brutality of South American soldiery in general, I accept his story.

There was another guy who came round to the club selling Panamanian seamen's union cards, which he said were neccesary to obtain work with certain companies whose ships flew the Panamanian flag. By this time my week's expected stay in New York was up, and the Orion ship due in Seattle had run aground and was a total loss. I joined this funny union and noticed on the back of the card that one could not be a Communist and be a member of the union. Later I heard that the union was completely spurious and that the organisers simply pocketed the dues and used the anti-Communist hysteria as a cover for their fraud. During this time I had to renew my U.S. visa which entailed a visit to the immigration office in Columbus Circle.

This is in a very beautiful part of New York City at the top of Central Park and I have very pleasnt memories of walking back through the Park in the spring sunshine admiring the apartments of the rich and famous. The immigration officials would demand to see proof of an offered job which would be supplied by the shipping company and they would stamp the visa for another week. This relentless bureaucracy seemed pointless to me as I read of Mexicans slipping over the border in thousands every day and the authorities being powerless to stop it. With ease of travel now, all of South America seems on the move over the Mexican border, so much so that a majority of Americans will be Latins by the end of the century. I am quite sure that they won't be prepared to do 'stoop' labour for poor pay by that time, so I would say there will be class conflict in the U.S. which, having a racial base, will be much more intense and bitter than ever happened in Europe. I made friends with an Australian girl who went to the M.N. club and whose father had been a general in the Australian army. Daddy must have provided the marvellous apartment she had in the same building as Marilyn Monroe. The apartment was in an oldish building which had been beautifully constructed at the turn of the century with sweeping stone staircases on either side of the lift shaft. I never got to see Marilyn Monroe but I did get to see American television, and later got to taste fish fingers which were new at the time.

One of the great features of New York City is the proliferation of theatres both on and off Broadway and I was privileged to see the wonderful O'Casey play 'Purple Dust', which had never been performed in Ireland.

This was performed in Greenwich Village which at the time had a reputation for homosexual contacts, but I found in the theatre all the accents of Ireland and saw some actors that had been in our own Group Theatre in Belfast. This was the theatre world of New York which was light years away from the maritime milieu in which I was moving.

Another time I went on a blind date with a girl of Hungarian descent who was very decent and wholesome. My English friend and myself both donned our uniforms and went out to the suburb of Queens to a night club where we entertained our two ladies. It was St Patrick's night so I wore a shamrock on my British Merchant Navy uniform just like the Irish Guards. I remembered having a lot to drink that night and getting back to Grand Central Station after the last subway train had gone. I walked from midtown Manhattan to the Battery on the tip of the island at 2 a.m. Walking through those man-made caverns to the sound of my own footsteps was an eerie experience. I would pass an odd drunk, and I remember two coloured men slagging off a drunken white who was trying to be patronising. At the very end of the two hour walk I reached the Bowery where the wino's slept out in shop doorways. One of them reached out his hand in a begging gesture. Other than this I was unmolested the whole time. It is an experience which would be very foolhardy to emulate at the present day in New York where crime is endemic. I have heard of people now being mugged in New York as they ran from their taxi to their hotel door.

I had now been in New York for one month, carousing every night and sitting around in the 'Doghouse' during the day with no word of a job either from Orion or the United Fruit Co. I was bored and depressed, as I think work is a neccesary ingredient for mental health. However, as so often in life, everything comes at once. Orion offered me a passage home on one of their ships bringing coal from Norfolk, Virginia to Rotterdam, so I decided that I would return and arrange to go to Poland to marry the girl who had written to me for two years. I was worried that I was becoming a sea gipsy as the Greeks called it, one without roots, without a home, and without even a homeland. Having lived with the denizens of the 'Doghouse' for a month I didn't want to become like them. Also I thought I could always come back to New York if I wanted. As fate would have it, the night before I was due to entrain for Norfolk a telegram arrived at the 'Doghouse' from United Fruit to join one of their ships at Baton Rouge, Louisiana at a salary of $600 a month, which today would be about $5000 a month.

I lay awake all night and weighed up the options and decided not to be a sea gipsy and return home. I told my English R.O. friend to ring United Fruit and offer his services but I am sure the Port Captain had a list of men available for such a job. I have of course had many regrets since as my proposed marriage came to nothing and I had a difficult time swallowing the anchor, but I didn't go back to sea for fourteen years and then it was as skipper of my own fishing vessel, but that's another story.

I took about ten men from my old ship down to Norfolk on the night train and joined a new bulk carrier as a passenger, only to find that the R.O. was a young Dublin guy who had just received a letter from home to say his father was seriously ill. I told him I would work the ship back to Rotterdam and the company could fly him home on compassionate grounds, which they did.

The journey home was uneventful except that the cook on this ship was a Communist who had been in a Greek Royalist government concentration camp. The camp was on an island without water and he told me the prisoners had to carry rocks from one end of the island to the other and then carry them back again. Because of the water shortage the prisoners were only given water to rinse their mouths during the lunchtime but had to spit it out again to be used on the governor's garden. The cook spoke good English and told me he had been educated by lawyers and professors, some of the best brains in Greece, who were also detained as Communists on the island. He made me porridge and boiled egg specially, as he knew that my diet would be different, and in every respect he was a humane and decent man.

We docked in Rotterdam and soon I was on my way to Belfast which then seemed to be a sleepy backwater on the edge of Europe but was, unfortunately, to become the focus of the world in its political travails. It was not easy to adapt to lower wages, self-catering and the sameness of shore life but I did it and when I think of my seafaring days I say to myself it was good, because I was young, and I would do it all over again and advise any young man to do the same.

I did meet the steward off the Okeanis when I was on holiday in Andros about ten years later. He told me the ship had sunk off County Clare in Ireland, that same county where my father was born.

The wheel had come full circle.